Eco

/ˈiːkəʊ/

adjective

1. ecological or environmental

2. not harmful to the environment

"the eco resort had no air conditioning and solar heated showers"

Copyright © 2016

All rights reserved. No part of this publication may be reproduced, stored in a retrieval system or transmitted in any form by any means without the prior permission of the copyright owner. Enquiries should be made to the publisher.

Every effort has been made to ensure that this book is free from error or omissions. However, the Publisher, the Author, the Editor or their respective employees or agents, shall not accept responsibility for injury, loss or damage occasioned to any person acting or refraining from action as a result of material in this book whether or not such injury, loss or damage is in any way due to any negligent act or omission, breach of duty or default on the part of the Publisher, the Author, the Editor, or their respective employees or agents.

The Author, the Publisher, the Editor and their respective employees or agents do not accept any responsibility for the actions of any person - actions which are related in any way to information contatinted in this book.
The moral right of the author has been asserted.

National Library of Australia Cataloguing-in-Publication entry

Author: Doak, Amy

Title: Eco Homes Of The World

ISBN: 9780994412683

Subject: Interior Decoration, Sustainable Architecture, Travel

Dewey Number: 728.37

Images by agreement with photographers. Please see page 124 for credits. The publisher has done its utmost to attribute the copyright holders of all the visual materials used. If you nevertheless think that a copyright has been infringed, please contact the publisher.

Published by:
Of The World Publishing
PO Box 8070
BENDIGO SOUTH LPO VIC 3550

www.oftheworldbooks.com

Eco Homes
of the world

Contents

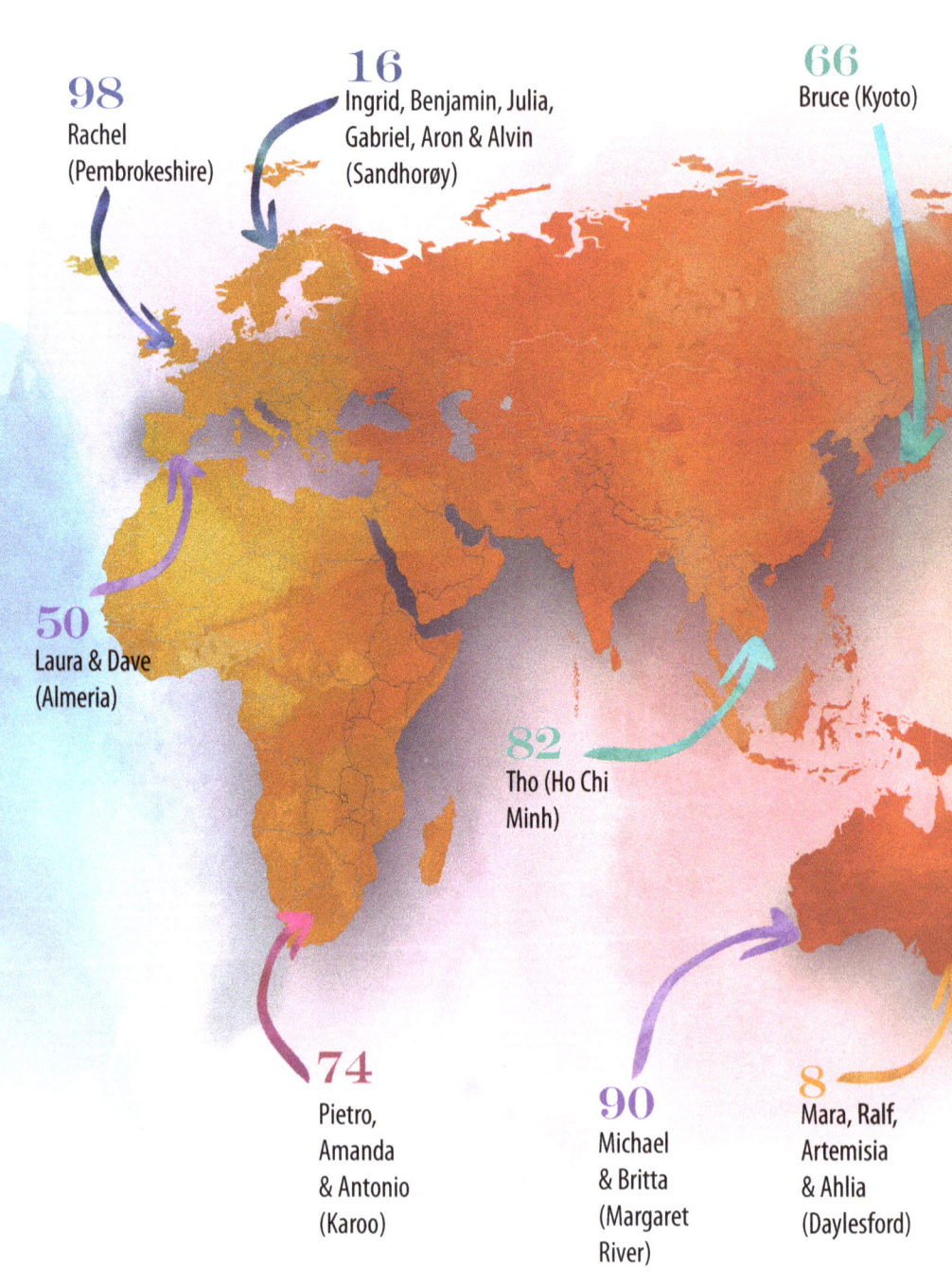

98 Rachel (Pembrokeshire)

16 Ingrid, Benjamin, Julia, Gabriel, Aron & Alvin (Sandhorøy)

66 Bruce (Kyoto)

50 Laura & Dave (Almeria)

82 Tho (Ho Chi Minh)

74 Pietro, Amanda & Antonio (Karoo)

90 Michael & Britta (Margaret River)

8 Mara, Ralf, Artemisia & Ahlia (Daylesford)

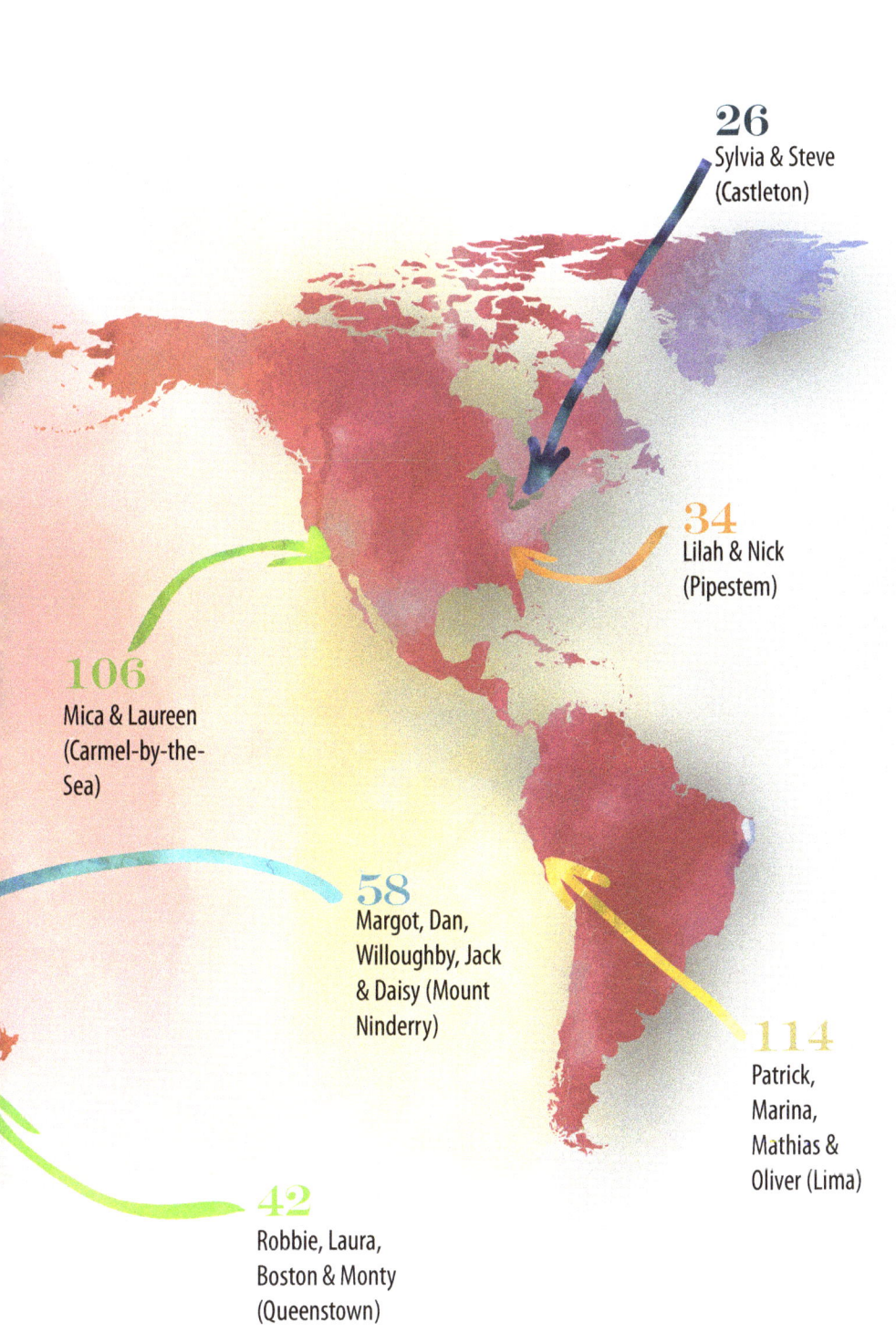

Introduction

We all have the ability to make the world a better place.

There's a lot of pressure when you say you want to lead a sustainable life, or live in an environmentally-friendly way. Many people expect that you will give away all your worldly possessions, never use technology again and only eat what you grow. Well, that's okay for some but it's not always realistic. The definition of an 'eco home' is varied and pliable.

For some, it's about sourcing materials that are abundant in the area and working with what is available. For others, it's about creating a space that won't draw on precious natural resources in the future. Or perhaps it's both of those things. Perhaps it's just working hard to be as good you can, in the place that you are in right now. Like we all are.

In discovering these homes, I've also discovered people who are passionate about the world and people who are keen to leave the planet in a better state than they found it. They may live in cities, rural areas, deserts or islands but they all have the same vision and offer the same advice:

Start small, just do what you can.

Shop local. Buy less.

Buy food that is in season and grown nearby (in your backyard even).

Be conscious of how much water you use.

Turn off appliances when you're not using them.

It's simple advice that we all know, yet we don't always follow.

You don't have to live in a cave in the middle of nowhere to be 'green' (although, as you will see ahead, it's fine if you do!) because by taking a small step, or by opening your eyes to alternative ways of living, you begin to change and you begin to make better choices. As one of our homeowners observes about their sustainable life: "if environmental awareness is a fundamental value, one doesn't feel compromised, because no other choice is appealing."

Whether you are looking to build an eco home of your own, or just looking for ways to live in a more environmentally friendly way, let these 14 people be your guide. Living in different countries and climates with many different challenges, they all have the same dream: to make our planet a wonderful place to live for many generations to come.

Daylesford, Australia
Mara, Ralf, Artemisia & Ahlia

In the state of Victoria and the Shire of Hepburn, around 115km north west of Melbourne, is the beautiful spa town of Daylesford. Established in 1852 as a gold mining town, Daylesford is known for its natural mineral spas and is the location of over 80 per cent of Australia's effervescent mineral water reserve. The township has a population of just under 3,000 yet sees over 1.6 million people visit on day trips each year.

In 2012, the Hepburn Shire Council launched an environmental sustainability strategy to promote and encourage sustainable use of resources, reduce fossil fuels and encourage diversity and prosperity in the region whilst enhancing and preserving the natural and built environment. With many passionate environmental activists living in the region, this small community is working towards a positive future.

Mara apologises. "It's not complete yet. We've still got a long way to go."

Anyone who tackles the mammoth task of building their own place must relate to this statement, but perhaps people who create an environmentally-friendly home even more so.

Not so long ago, Mara, Ralf and their two daughters lived in a little 1950s house in Melbourne. Mara admits that their Melbourne home was very cosy. "Ralf had renovated the house with passive solar design, so it was warm with lovely natural light. It was small so it was easy to clean and extremely comfortable. We had a productive garden and a chicken run, but five years ago Ralf had explained he really wanted to live in the country. I promised him that by the age of 40, if our expenses allowed, we would look to buy a slice of it."

Around that time Mara, a performer who migrated from Italy to Australia when she was nine, was singing Italian songs as part of the Boite Singers Festival in Daylesford. "At the end of the festival,

Ralf and I looked at various properties. Some were too big, some were bordered by large power lines. Others were too small, or thick with forest and no solar access." Then, they found a 15-acre paddock in Blampied with beautiful views of Mount Franklin and they knew they'd found home.

"It was all about the people," Mara says of the location. "Daylesford is pretty and has gorgeous gardens and deciduous trees that change colour from green to very bright red, but its aesthetic appeal would have soon lost its beauty had the community here not been as beautiful. It is a very beautiful community. Caring, kind, open, bright and looking to challenge the world to be a better place for all. The permaculture movement is strong here, thanks to two very bright stars – David Holmegren and Sue Dennet. This is a movement that has always captured my imagination. It is deeply interested in human health and planet health."

When it came to creating the perfect home, Mara says the right land was very important. "We needed it to have excellent solar access. Size was also an important factor; it needed to be small enough that we could financially manage it in the long term. When it came to creating the house, the most important features had to do with the building envelope – windows, light, earth walls, slab and greenhouse. Sometimes you can end up with a beautiful house that costs a great deal to maintain and once its beauty has settled you almost stop seeing it because you are so disgruntled with its poor performance in terms of comfort. We are now close to the start of winter and I wake up in the morning and my room is warm. The double glazed windows are keeping the cool air out. The walls, which are straw mixed with a small amount of clay and rendered, are a thermal break from the winter chill. The slab, a thick thermal mass, has absorbed the heat of the day and is slowly releasing it back. Our north-facing greenhouse creates a pocket of warm air in the downstairs bathroom and in the living room.

"In our upstairs bathroom we have a very simple and clever detail. The combustion-stove flue is bent to ensure a passage through the room. When the fire is lit, the heat is not lost to the roof cavity, but captured by the bathroom. There is only one combustion heater in the house and it heats the first and second floor in just a few hours."

Mara says some of her friends were going through a conventional build at the same time they started their home and it's been interesting to compare. "I think what we've done compares favourably," she says. "The light-earth build is an excellent choice for urban areas too. For those who feel that straw bale building takes up too much of the home's footprint, light-earth solves that problem because with light-earth you tear the bales apart, wet them and mix them with a small quantity of clay. Then, you press them into formwork around a contemporary stud frame. This method of building is quite rare in Australia and it's very labour intensive, however if it were taken up by mainstream builders, I can easily imagine cement trucks appropriated to mix large quantities of straw, clay and water for the mixed content to be poured in to formwork, which would reduce the hardest part of the build.

"The value of this process is that, unlike conventional building, the insulation and the building fabric are all one product. This means you avoid the very real situation that many people face with shoddy insulation installations, with gaps that let heat in during summer and trap it. If there are gaps in your wall due to the light-earth mix not adequately pressed in, you can see the hole clearly and can patch it up with more of the mix when the formwork is removed."

When it comes to making a difference, Mara says the best thing you can do is simply start. "Start by planting your first herb, then your second, then a lemon tree, then an apricot tree, then a quince.

Start by inviting friends to cook with you and ask them to bring ingredients they have bought from a place other than a supermarket. Start by carrying a small, reusable, easy-to-squish bag in your handbag and refusing plastic ones. Start with a bushwalk with your local wilderness society. Start by growing a vine along the façade of your home, by not concreting your backyard, or your front yard, or your carpark. Get rid of your carport, plant a garden and park on the street instead. Start by planting a tree on your nature strip, then a small shrub and maybe some wildflowers. More than anything we need more trees, more shrubs, more wildflowers, more luscious, sensual, visually-inspiring, uplifting and oxygen-producing green!"

Mara and Ralf have ensured their new home is far more environmentally-friendly than many houses built today, but she still questions whether there is more they can do. "Our home has solar hot water and a five kilowatt solar system to reduce electricity and therefore greenhouse gases; we have a 220,000 litre rainwater tank to reduce our reliance on bore water; our sewage run-off feeds our plants and we are re-vegetating our site and providing habitat for local wildlife. We are motivated and passionate and doing our best but we are also craving a change away from government policies that are short-term. However, can any of us say we are living an environmentally-friendly life when we are all still relying on fossil fuels for all the products we access? We like to say we are working towards, advocating and celebrating an environmentally-friendly life!

For now, Mara and Ralf will continue to create their home as best as they know how. "This house is much bigger than our old home because I want to run kitchen garden workshops once it's finished. It needs to accommodate a group of 10 easily around the island bench for baking bread, making fresh pasta, fermenting, preserving. We have yet to make furniture for the house, yet to build bookshelves for all our deeply-loved books. The vegetable garden and chicken run are yet to be made, so for now it's a house on its way to being a home." And a very beautiful house at that.

Learn more about Mara and Ralf's journey by visiting their website: www.villagedreaming.com.au

"Daylesford is very pretty, but its aesthetic appeal would have soon lost its beauty had the community here not been as beautiful."

Sandhorøy, Norway
Ingrid, Benjamin, Julia, Gabriel, Aron & Alvin

Norway has long been known as a global leader in environmentally-friendly policies, however in recent months it's gone even one step further – with the pledge to become 100 per cent climate neutral by 2030, two decades earlier than planned. Following a vote that made Norway the first nation in the world to ban public procurements that contribute to rainforest destruction, this latest announcement is yet another way in which Norway is leading the world.

In the northwestern coast of the Scandinavian Peninsula in northern Norway you will find the county of Nordland. Despite its high latitude, the region has a relatively mild climate with an average temperature of four degrees Celsius. With rich marine life, spruce and birch forests and an abundance of endemic birds and animals, the region is also home to seven National Parks. Sandhorøy is a mountainous island on the west coast of Nordland with a population of just over 200. It's a place of great natural beauty.

If ever there was a magical place to connect with nature, surely it's on a little island at the top of the world where a glass roof will give you the most perfect view of the Northern Lights. For Ingrid and her family, this is everyday life.

"We got the inspiration and idea to build in late 2010," Ingrid says. "We started building in the spring of 2012 and we had moved in by December 2013."

This may seem to many like a fairly speedy process for such an unusual home, but Ingrid credits

the enthusiasm of the local government and also their rigourous pre-planning that allowed the relatively stress-free build to occur. "The land we have is beautiful – seven kilometres square, right on the beach," says Ingrid of their location. "Where we live is pretty, clean and quiet. Both Benjamin and I grew up here and we have family here. We didn't have too many issues building the house. We did a lot of work ahead of time to ensure that all questions were answered, but the local government liked the idea and they were keen to see it built."

"Norway is considered to be one of the best places in the world to live, and I think I have to agree – particularly living where we do. It's very peaceful here, the environment is clean and the standard of living is high. We try to do the things we love and feel inspired to do, and this house is definitely a visual example of that. We built exactly what we wanted."

What they wanted was essentially a house in a very large and beautiful greenhouse. Living in a part of the world that can get very cold, windy, wet and snowy, the cob house is covered in a large dome that enables the family of six to live 'outdoors', year round. "The house is made from wood, clay, sand and straw, cob and strawbale," Ingrid explains. "We have many vegetables and fruit trees on our land and we are trying to grow more each year, but we have a very short summer season here in the Arctic Circle. With the dome and our automatic water treatment system – which waters and gives nutrients to our greenhouse plants with all our waste water – we are able to grow organic fruits and vegetables year round.

"Heating is from the sun, both directly and from solar collectors, and these heat the water we use and the radiant floor heating water. In winter, we are in the shade for three months so the fireplace heats the house and the water, with electricity as back up."

Ingrid says that although her family has always had an interest in the environment and eco-

friendly living, they found that they started getting a little more serious when building started. "Our lifestyle has changed gradually," she says. "But we cannot use anything except for biodegradable household products now due to our water system. Everything we use, eat or flush comes back to us as a tomato or an apple! In saying that though, there is nothing that we've given up because of the house. We built it to fit us and our lives."

Ingrid says that by doing most of the work themselves, they were able to create exactly what they wanted, and save money in the process. "The house is about half the price of a normal house the same size, if it had been built by contractors. We built this house ourselves, but included some expensive features such as the glass dome and the heating system. Most people who are looking at building could do the same but it does take some DIY skills and a lot of self-effort if it is to be cheaper than a regular house."

As well as raising their young family, Ingrid works as a nurse and Benjamin is a fish farmer, but the pair have recently started their own company – Hjertefølger AS – which offers classes, workshops and retreats on yoga, natural building, natural birth, vegan cooking and raw food. They also host viewings of their unique home and cater for tourists. Ingrid has found that sharing their journey has been a wonderful way to inspire others to live in a sustainable way.

Still, she says there are ways that they could always improve. "We live far away from everything, so we use a car more than we would like to," she admits. "However, you don't have to build a new house, or move to an island, to live an eco-friendly life. There are many little things that people can do to make a difference to the world. Eat an organic and plant-based diet. Buy less stuff. Grow more food. Share."

You can follow Ingrid, Benjamin and the journey of their amazing space and lives on www.naturhuset.blogg.no

"Our lifestyle changed gradually but now, due to our water system, everything we use, eat or flush comes back to us as a tomato or an apple!"

Castleton, Canada
Sylvia & Steve

Canada is the second-largest country in the world, after Russia. Home to the world's largest proportion of fresh water lakes, it also has the longest coastline to protect. Much of its land is dominated by forest, tundra and the Rocky Mountains. That's a lot of environment to be responsible for. In 2008, the government passed the Federal Sustainable Development Act showing its commitment to sustainable development. Updated every three years, the Act pushes the government to take environmental issues seriously.

On the north shore of Lake Ontario, in the east-central Canadian state of Ontario, you will find Northumberland County. Despite Ontario being the country's most populous state, Northumberland is a pretty, quiet region surrounded by natural beauty. The small rural community of Castleton is approximately 140 kilometres from Toronto offering residents the perfect mix of farming and city life.

When many people retire they take the opportunity to put their feet up, or perhaps travel the world. Sylvia and Steve, however, are two retired high school teachers who built their own rammed earth home, then started a company to help others do the same. One would think that years teaching high school is enough time spent hoping to change the world but, as Sylvia explains, there's plenty more to be done.

"We believe in trying to make the world a better place," Sylvia says. "In building a sustainable house, we wanted to employ a method that would drastically reduce the carbon footprint of the process. Our research led us to believe that rammed earth is the most sustainable method of building today. We were also impressed by its many other benefits – such as its beauty, acoustical qualities, health benefits and fire-resistant qualities.

"Since living in this home we have appreciated its comfort; the individual beauty of each rammed earth wall, the cosy feeling of being completely protected from weather and noise, the constant temperature and humidity of the dust-free air all contribute to the feeling of well-being. Even the guitars stay in tune."

When they were starting out, Sylvia and Steve enlisted the support of sustainable award-winning architect, Terrell Wong (pictured with Sylvia on page 26), of Stone's Throw Design Inc. "It was an excellent starting point for our rammed earth project. She was able to use a variety of approaches that maximised the low-tech, passive solar and passive ventilation possibilities of building with rammed earth. The stunning design of the house helps bring it close to Passive House standards, which will save us money for the rest of our lives."

The project was such a success that the couple went on to create a business – educating others about the benefits of rammed earth homes and working with people to build a home of their own. "Because we feel passionately about bringing rammed earth to everyone, we have enlisted Terrell again to design a modest gabled bungalow with a loft that we hope to build for about the same price as a comparable stick frame house, but with all the advantages of rammed earth."

Rammed earth walls are constructed by ramming a mixture of aggregates – gravel, sand, silt and a small amount of clay – into place between flat panels, or formwork. Traditional methods involved ramming the end of a wooden pole into the earth mixture to compress it – modern technology makes use of a mechanical ram. Sometimes known as pisé walls, the method has seen buildings around the globe stand strong for many years. In Lyon, France, there are rammed earth buildings dating as far back as 1562.

"Several times a week I have a conversation with someone inquiring about the feasibility of using rammed earth construction," Sylvia admits. "Drawing from our experiences with this house, I am able to assure them of rammed earth's capacity to withstand multiple freeze/thaw cycles, be used underground and built several stories high, eliminate the need for air conditioning and drastically lower the need for supplementary heating. We have frequent visitors and it is always interesting to see the shift in thinking as they realise this is not a 'mud hut' but very much a mainstream building

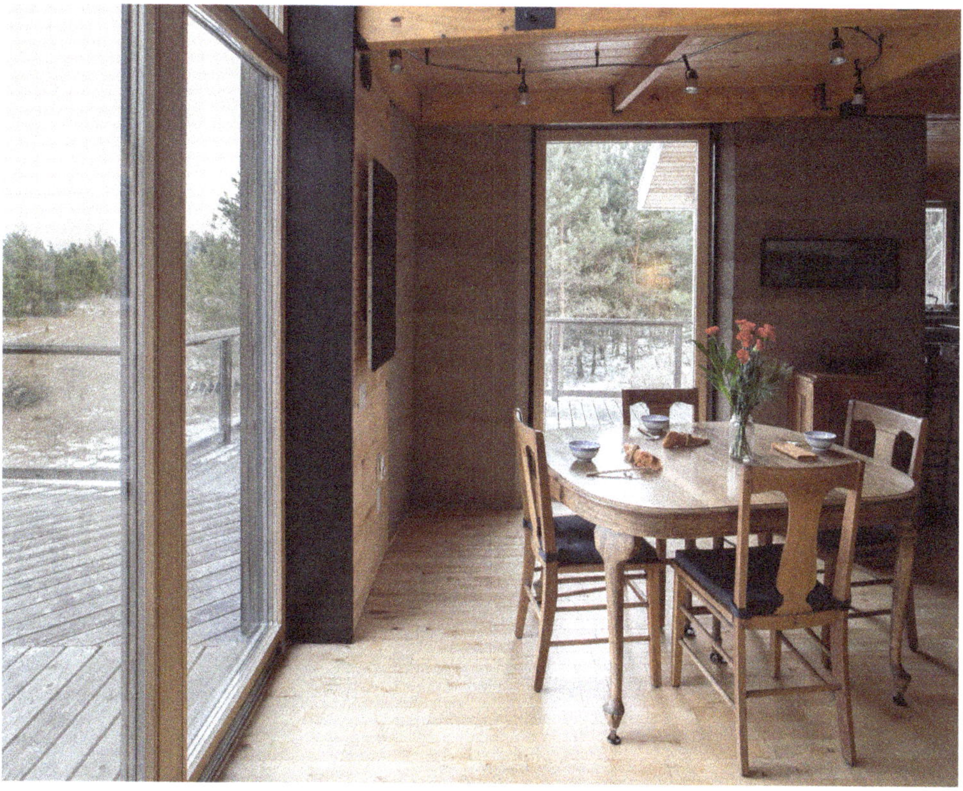

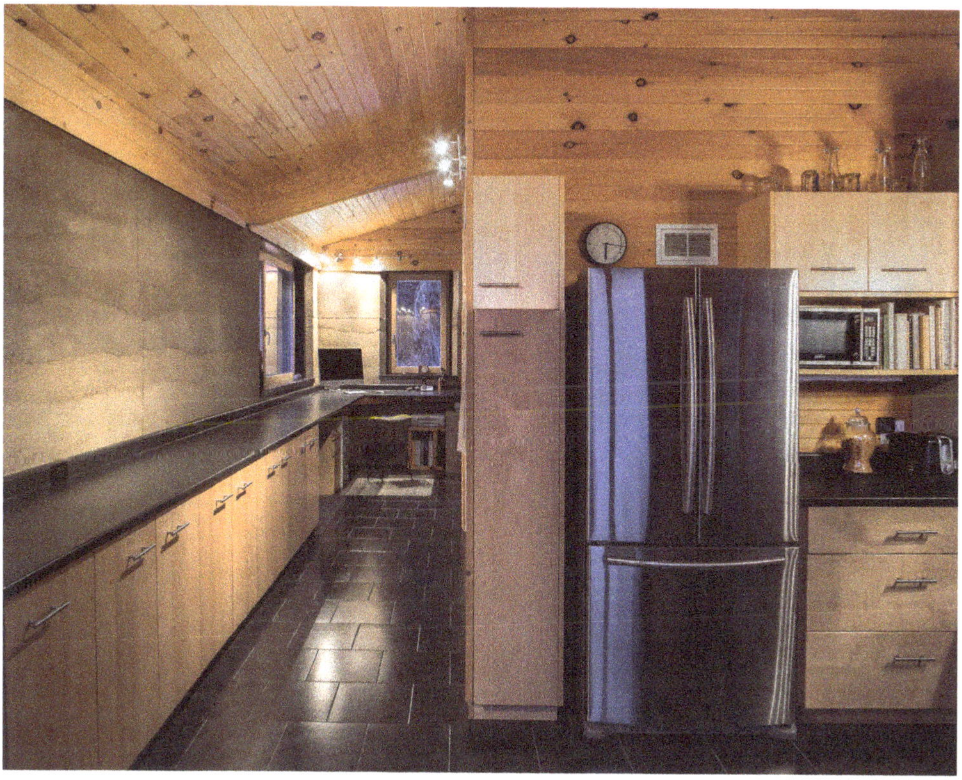

system with upscale potential. A large part of the 'wow' factor is Terrell's brilliant design, but the rammed earth is definitely an attraction. For many, the extreme energy efficiency and sustainability are merely a bonus.

"The key sustainable attributes of rammed earth are its low embodied energy and its thermal mass. The planet cannot afford the environmental price of current building practices — from clear-cutting to provide wood, to the huge carbon footprint of concrete. Beyond the construction phase, rammed earth excels in providing airtight, energy-efficient buildings with ample thermal mass to store passive solar energy. Even in the cold winters and hot humid summers of Ontario we have neither furnace nor air conditioner.

"Northumberland County has beautiful rolling hills and is close to Toronto with easy access to a number of small Ontario cities. It has a nice mix of rural and urban sensibilities. Our little lot was largely a monoculture of pines when we bought it and it has been fun watching diversity develop as other species move in. The local building inspector was mostly curious after assuring herself that a competent structural engineer oversaw the project. A long-term goal of ours is to have rammed earth introduced into the Ontario Building Code."

Sylvia says she was an environmentalist long before it was 'cool'. "It's weirdly nice to find my values becoming mainstream," she laughs. "Everything we do has environmental consequences, many of which are difficult to fully unpack. The best that any of us can do is simply make do with less. Beyond that, we need to look at every decision in the light of its impacts on the larger environment. Collectively we need to be focusing on building resiliency into our societies, cultures and infrastructures, which is why I feel it is important to build as much with rammed earth as possible with a long-term goal of influencing the built environment.

"Canada is a fantastic country to live in, with gorgeous landscapes and seasons as well as people who are stereotypically polite. If we can bring enough political pressure to bear to switch our economy from resource extraction to green innovation, I have optimism that our traditional peace-keeping roles can expand to being a beacon of sustainability for the world."

Learn more about Sylvia's rammed earth homes at www.aerecura.ca

"The individual beauty of each rammed earth wall, the cosy feeling of being protected from the weather and noise, the constant temperature...all contribute to the feeling of well-being."

Pipestem, USA
Lilah & Nick

West Virginia is a state located in the Appalachian region to the east of the United States. With a population of over 1.8 million, West Virginia is considered one of the smaller states. It's known just as much for its natural beauty (John Denver referred to it as 'almost heaven' in his song *Take Me Home, Country Roads*) as it is for its mining in coal, oil and gas.

As the rest of the country looks towards a future that depends less on coal and more on renewable energy, there are changes in store for the region whether they like it or not. An emphasis on tourism is continuing to grow – it is now one of the state's largest industries – and much of this is focused around nature. The Appalachian Trail, as well as beautiful national parks, mountain ranges and valleys, are drawing outdoor enthusiasts from all over the world. To the very south of the state is one of the smaller, yet very beautiful, state parks: Pipestem. With scenic vistas, mountains and rivers, the region is surrounded by a community of growers and makers, keen to preserve its natural beauty.

Lilah and Nick are artists and much of their life is about creating in some way, shape or form. So, it makes perfect sense their first home together would evolve in much the same way. Lilah, who makes ceramics and works for a clothing company developing solutions for the third life of their product, and Nick, who makes tin type photographs and works as a carpenter, started creating their home almost by accident.

"The land belongs to Nick's family," Lilah explains of their space in the south of West Virginia. "It has been passed down for many generations. We built our little place on the top of the hill there because we so badly wanted to create a space for ourselves."

The plan to build was a little dream the pair had on their very first date! Nick brought Lilah to the spot they have since built on, to watch the sun set over the West Virginian mountains. They both agreed it would be beautiful to create a house just meant for watching sunsets and they drew a little sketch. Of course, you can't watch a beautiful sunset from one tiny window…and so the concept of a wall of windows was created!

"It was actually very cheap to create the home," Lilah says. "We used mostly salvaged materials, a lot of which came from an old cattle barn that we took down on the other side of the property. We spent a lot of time searching garage sales and antique stores for the windows and other bits and pieces. We did all the labour ourselves, which saved us a huge amount of money. I think most people could afford to do this type of project, so long as they had the time to do it themselves, and the space to build on. We were very lucky to have both."

Lilah admits she was a novice when they started building but Nick, with formal training in log building and construction, gave them a good basis to start with. "We learnt from books and watching little videos," Lilah says. "We would drive to town and sit in the library reading books on shed construction, then go to a café and watch YouTube videos. It's surprising how quickly you learn."

Tackling the wall of windows ended up being more about leaning on their artistic sensibilities. Nick created a solid post and beam frame for support, and then the pair went ahead with what was essentially one giant jigsaw puzzle. "We started out trying to use math and making a plan, but neither of those things are our strong suit," Lilah laughs. "Basically, we ended up winging it and it worked out perfectly! I would definitely recommend trusting your instinct…and perhaps not screwing everything in right away."

Lilah and Nick don't live in the home permanently, but they live simply and sustainably when they are there. "There is no electricity. No running water. No gas," Lilah says. "We heat the house with a tiny wood stove and cut the wood from the forest the house sits in. We use candles and simply go to bed when it gets dark out! We cook on a campfire and we use water from a nearby well. We mostly use it as a summer cabin now so it's about as sustainable as long-term camping. We designed the

house to heat itself passively from the sun and there is a great cross-breeze that cools the place when you open up all the doors and windows.

"Because it doesn't have power or water, most of the 'unsustainable' items that we would covet wouldn't even work there. It's actually really nice to take the time to make your coffee in the morning on a wood stove or over the campfire. Everything takes longer – which isn't always easy and patience is a hard thing to learn. However, we are motivated to change our lifestyle and do our small part for the world."

Despite the unique beauty of their little home, Lilah says it's the location that makes it all the more special. "It really does come down to community. The land can be beautiful, but without friends or family to share it with, it never quite 'sticks' as home. Also, the land was really the biggest factor in making this a sustainable project. West Virginia is a rural enough place that we didn't require special permits. Essentially, the cabin is a shed!

"Both Nick and I have always had a connection to the land we live on. Nick was raised on a small farm in Wisconsin and my mother is a gardener, so growing up we were both always working the land. It seems more important than ever these days to stay connected to your environment and work to live as sustainably as possible.

"I think the best exercise in realising how wasteful we are as a society is to carry around all the trash you make in the course of a week. It's amazing how much we don't need. From there, you can certainly begin to learn ways to lessen your impact and change habits, spaces, homes and lives."

When it comes to making the world a better place, building a home or just creating something new, perhaps Nick sums it up the best when he says, "If you have an idea, you can find a way to make it." If you ever needed proof that statement is true, you will find it in this little pocket of West Virginia.

To discover more about Lilah and her work, check out www.lilahhorwitz.com or the couple's blog at www.oldworldgrange.tumblr.com

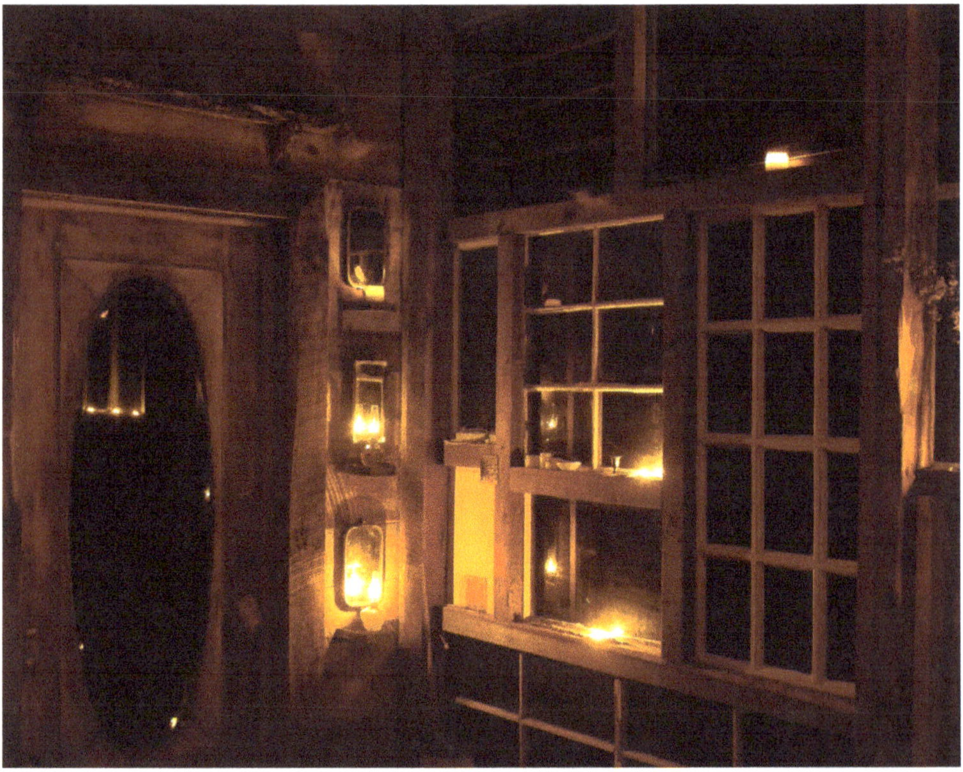

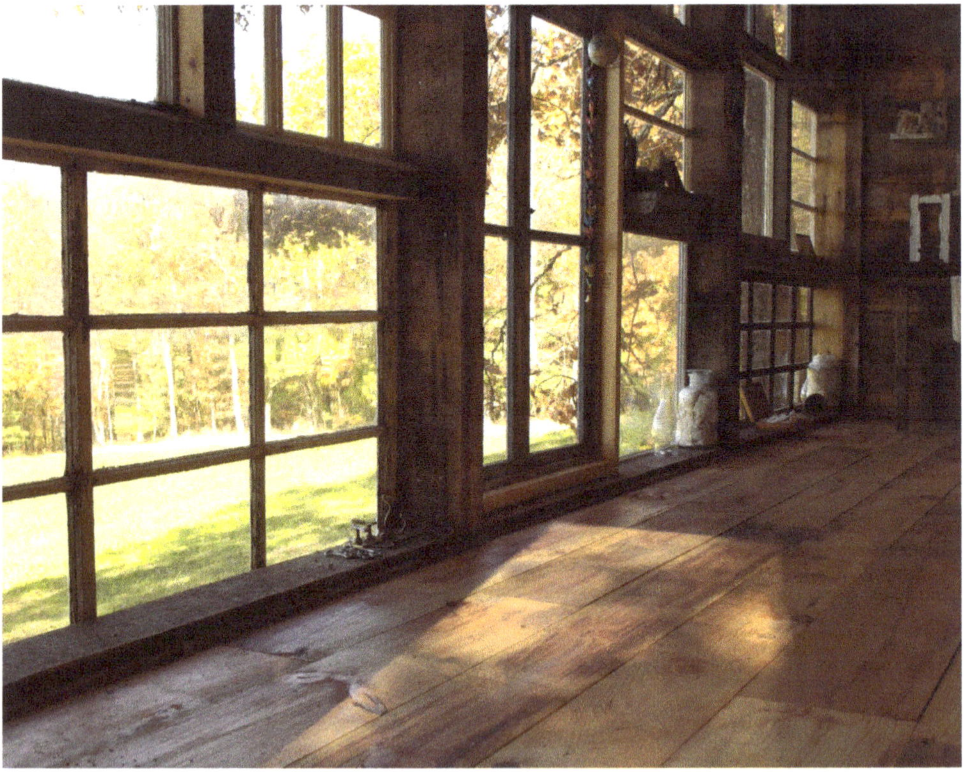

"I think most people could afford to do this type of project, so long as they had the time to do it themselves, and the space to build on. We were very lucky to have both."

Queenstown, New Zealand
Robbie, Laura, Boston & Monty

In the south island of New Zealand, sitting alongside the shore of Lake Wakatipu and the Southern Alps you will find Queenstown. With a population of just over 30,000 the area is known for its pinot noir and chardonnay vineyards and for every adventure sport you can imagine. From skiing in winter to paragliding, mountain biking and bungee jumping in summer, there is certainly no excuse to say you're bored here.

Outside of the action – there are plenty of beautiful restaurants and a great arts scene here also – you will find the real splendor. New Zealand is known for its gorgeous scenery and Queenstown is surrounded by it. The country has great respect for this natural beauty with the government working towards targets of 90 per cent renewable energy by the year 2025. Whilst there are still issues – as with all first-world nations – about living a sustainable life, it appears that New Zealand is certainly a country that is, as a whole, aware of what needs to change in order to help make the world a better place.

After looking to buy an existing home in Queenstown, Robbie and his family started to think that perhaps it would be more affordable to purchase a section of land and build their own place. Robbie, an architectural designer, and Laura, an illustrator, had the perfect combination of knowledge and imagination to be able to create a beautiful and functional eco-friendly family home.

"We'd always wanted to build, but we didn't know if it was feasible for our first home," Robbie says. "However, when we found the perfect section on the edge of an established subdivision we saw

it as the perfect opportunity to create a small, energy-efficient home for our family. Once we'd secured the land, it all came together relatively easy. I designed the house with our young family in mind and also to suit our modest budget and Laura, as an artist, didn't want a house that looked the same as everyone else's."

After living in the home for two years, Robbie says that they're so happy with all of their choices – it couldn't be a more perfect home. "We wanted a warm, healthy, energy-efficient home for our family," he explains. "With harsh winters and hot summers, the best way to create a comfortable indoor environment was to concentrate on the building envelope first. The walls, roof and floor have almost double the minimum requirement for insulation, and thermal bridging has been minimized – including a fully insulated concrete slab.

"A high-tech airtightness membrane has been installed to the inside of the timber frame to minimize uncontrolled air filtration – which would reduce insulation performance – and eliminate any condensation build-up within the wall cavity, which can lead to mould. We wanted to ensure that we didn't use any toxic building materials and that included timber treatments or VOCs in paint or finishings. Although some materials are quite energy intensive to produce – like concrete and steel – they are also highly durable and last an extremely long time with minimal maintenance.

"We also incorporated passive solar design with north-facing windows and thermal mass to store the heat from the sun. Our power bills are very low and the house maintains a constant temperature of around 18 to 22 degrees celcius."

Robbie believes that setting out to create an eco home from the start ensured that the process wasn't any more expensive than a regular build. "Houses have been getting bigger and bigger over

the years and prices keep going up," he says. "The easiest way to build a more affordable and more energy-efficient home is to build smaller. We were also lucky in that we had a lot of friends happy to assist with parts of the build and this helped us come in under budget."

The result is a beautiful, modern home that very much reflects Robbie and Laura's desire to live in a sustainable way. "I have a background in environmental science and sustainable architecture and I really wanted to design and build a home that was true to our ethos."

Robbie, who runs a small design and draughting business, can now ensure his clients get the most of their brief when it comes to green building design. "It is sometimes a challenge to balance convenience and sustainability – in home design and everyday life," Robbie admits. "We have a large veggie garden and we're very conscious of where we spend our money and the kinds of companies that we support. I would always encourage people to start small. Just support local businesses. Buy ethically-produced goods. Grow some veggies."

Of course, there is no question that looking out your window at a beautiful mountain vista helps that sense of connection with the environment. Robbie agrees that the family is fortunate to reside in such a stunning pocket of the world. "We feel really lucky to live in such a beautiful place amongst scenic lakes and mountains," he says. "We love the outdoors and enjoy hiking, mountain biking, fishing as well as horse riding in the summer and snowboarding during the winter months.

"New Zealand is a great place to live. Outside of one major city – Auckland – the country is sparsely populated, especially down here in the south island. It hasn't been overdeveloped and the large number of National Parks means the pristine natural environment has been preserved. However, we aren't without our challenges. Extensive farming, introduced pests, mining for minerals, increasing population... we need to be aware of how quickly things can change. We perhaps need to take a little more care of our waterways, but I am quite proud that New Zealand is pretty 'clean and green.'"

With young families like Robbie's taking charge of the future, it seems that this is one part of the world that is in good hands.

"Houses have been getting bigger and bigger over the years and prices keep going up. The easiest way to build a more affordable and more energy-efficient home is to build smaller."

Almeria, Spain
Laura & Dave

In the very south of Spain is the city of Almeria. With a population of just under 200,000, the city was created in the 10th century as a medieval fortress. Now, it's known for its tourist attractions – centuries-old castles and pretty seaside promenades. One of the eight provinces of the region of Andalucia, Almeria and its surrounds witnessed a spectacular growth in the 1960s and 1970s. Unfortunately, it was based on economics above the environment and when the Environment Agency was established in 1984, the area had a great deal of work to do in order to reach the average level of other regions in the country.

Over the last 25 years, Andalucia has implemented an environmental structure that covers legislation, education, natural sites and species protection as well as rural development. With continued plans to grow a 'green' economy, the region is finally starting to catch up with the rest of the country and while there is much more that can be done, it is great to see the region headed in the right direction.

Laura's interest in the environment and eco-friendly living was actually inspired by TV. "Did you ever see that British comedy from the 70s called *The Good Life*?" she laughs. "I just loved that program and I am sure it fueled my eco habits! Of course, I am also very much in love with nature. Perhaps even more so since moving to Spain."

Laura, her partner, Dave, and their four rescue cats, live in a remote semi-desert region in rural Spain and since their arrival in 2002 they have been working hard to create their dream home – an earthship.

"Dave is a computer database programmer, but I think in a former life he must have been a bird because he loves to fly," Laura says. "He used to fly a hand glider, then he became a sky diver, then he

flew a microlight and a helicopter. He was born and brought up in Bogota, Colombia, and learnt a lot about engineering and general wood and metal working from his father. He's a fearless builder who is happy to take on anything necessary to complete the job. His parents ran a school in Bogota that was big and rambling and always needed repairs and when we moved here from the UK, he famously said, 'I just want to live in a house that's finished.' We've been in a constant state of renovating and building ever since!

"I am a mixed media and fibre artist…and perhaps a cat in a former life! I love taking life slowly and looking at the small, often overlooked, elements in nature. My design background has been a good fit with Dave's engineering experience – I look at problems from an aesthetic viewpoint and Dave sees them from a more practical angle."

Laura was born in Singapore and lived in Germany, Wales and then the south of England before moving to Spain and the decision to create an earthship wasn't the initial plan. "When we moved here, we started out renovating an old cortijo and then decided that its position on a country road wasn't the best considering the number of cats who were coming to live with us. It was then we decided to move and build our own eco-friendly dwelling. I found earthships on the internet and immediately fell in love with them. Dave agreed, and the rest, you could say, is history! I guess you could say that we built this earthship for our cats."

After a great deal of research, Laura and Dave bought the introductory earthship book and worked out what they needed in a piece of land. "The very first plot we were interested in – even though it was the third plot we saw – was the one we bought. We then contacted the local town hall to talk about planning permission."

This became a long and drawn out process, which Laura and Dave have gone on to share in their earthship book and on their website – www.earthship.es – and seven-and-a-half years later they finally received permission to live in their earthship as a proper home. "We still have a list as long as your arm of things that need to be done before we can call it finished," Laura says. "During the build we've had many volunteers with us and we've done a lot ourselves, but the time it's taken has actually been a bonus because it's allowed us to research alternative, more eco-friendly solutions and really just let it evolve.

"Our earthship is the first legal earthship in Spain – as far as we know. Definitely the first in Andalucia. We were totally committed to making it legal so it would open the doors for others who wanted to do the same. Despite hiccups along the way with the Provincial government, the timing was just right for us to complete it as we now have."

So, what is an earthship? "The basic principles of an earthship are that it's mainly built out of recycled and local materials and it uses the ground to equalise the internal temperatures of the home – a bit like a cave house," Laura explains. "Our house is actually called Cuevas de Sol (Caves of Sun) and is basically a cave house with a greenhouse on the front. The cave is created by tyre walls and earth berm at the back of the building, and the greenhouse lets in light and heat from the sun.

"The mass takes up the heat and releases it when the air gets cooler, equalising the temperatures. Our house ranges from between 15 to 32 degrees celcius when outside temperatures are from -2 to 46-plus degrees celcius. We don't need any back-up heating during winter and during summer our solar panels create so much electricity we are able to use a small air conditioner or fan. We are planning to shade the front face more next summer, which will help.

"Water is another neat feature – you catch it from your roof and use it four times which greatly reduces how much you need. The first time is for cooking or washing. This grey water is then fed into indoor planters and the roots of the plants clean it enough to be used to flush the toilets. The blackwater from the toilet is then cleaned in a septic tank and used outside for landscaping."

Laura says the cost of materials is relatively low compared to other types of building – especially if you upcyle doors, furniture and fittings like they have. "Costs do vary," she admits. "Timber is relatively cheap in America but very expensive here. We've had access to local cork for our insulation, something that wouldn't be easily available everywhere. My advice is to investigate what materials there is an abundance of in your area and work out how to use it!"

Laura and Dave's region is the only semi-desert area in Europe. "It has stunning scenery with huge skies and almost lunar-like landscapes," Laura says. "The variety of flora and fauna is incredible – I'm told this is because during the ice age the ice didn't come this far south so many species survived. As well as the scenery, we've also found a like-minded community nearby, with an organic veggie box farmer, artists of every kind and a permaculture group and others interested in an eco-friendly life.

Given the remoteness of where we are, this was a pleasant surprise!

"We've faced many challenges since moving here. There's rampant corruption in this country, which makes it hard to live here as an outsider. I would say though, that we've met so many lovely, kind and warm-hearted Spanish people, many of whom are dedicated to living an eco-friendly life.

"I don't think there is one thing that we miss about a conventional home. Living in an earthship is such a comfortable experience, like being hugged in a soft and gentle inspiring space. My idea of interior design has changed hugely since moving to Spain and moving into the earthship – I think for the better. The colour of mud is a very natural and warm colour to live with! A lot of our design ideas have come naturally as an answer to the needs of the interior layout. For instance, our washing up area has lots of open draining racks close to the sink. These racks are the permanent storage area for plates and cutlery – so no drying up needed – and they drain straight into the first stage planter, which, of course, is placed right next to the sink."

Despite Laura and Dave's efforts to live a 'green' life, she says there is always more that can be done. "The more I think about living in an environmentally-friendly way, the more I realise we have a long way to go. I do have to remind myself of how much we do now. At one of our open days, I mentioned where the satellite TV dish would go and one of the visitors was quite indignant when he said, 'TV? Shouldn't you greenies be reading books instead of watching TV?!' Another person I met was quite unimpressed when I couldn't tell him exactly what our carbon footprint would be once the earthship was built. Tiny wasn't an acceptable answer for him!

"The internet is a great source of information and there are thousands of ideas about starting an environmentally-friendly life, but some of my thoughts include: buy your food from local, organic suppliers; be aware of packaging and try to choose products with minimal packaging; eat foods in season; reduce your meat intake; make use of your council recycling services; use environmentally-friendly cleaning products; buy products from eco-friendly makers and embrace slow fashion. Start where you feel comfortable and make small changes – just one or two at a time."

Find out more about Laura and Dave's earthship journey by visiting their website, www.earthship.es

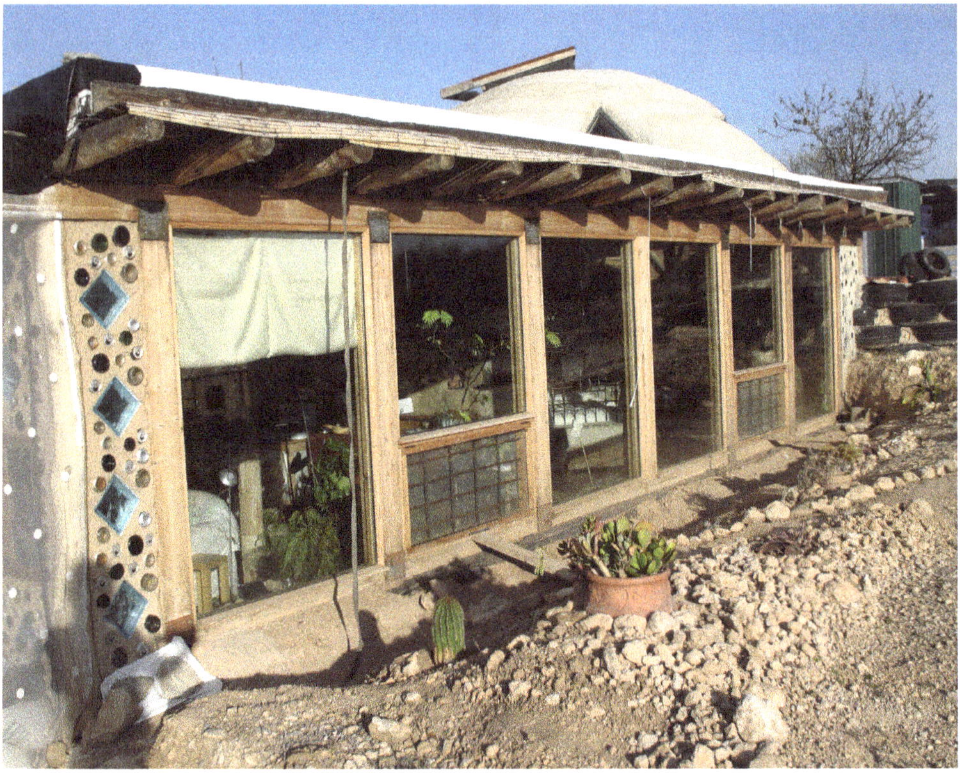

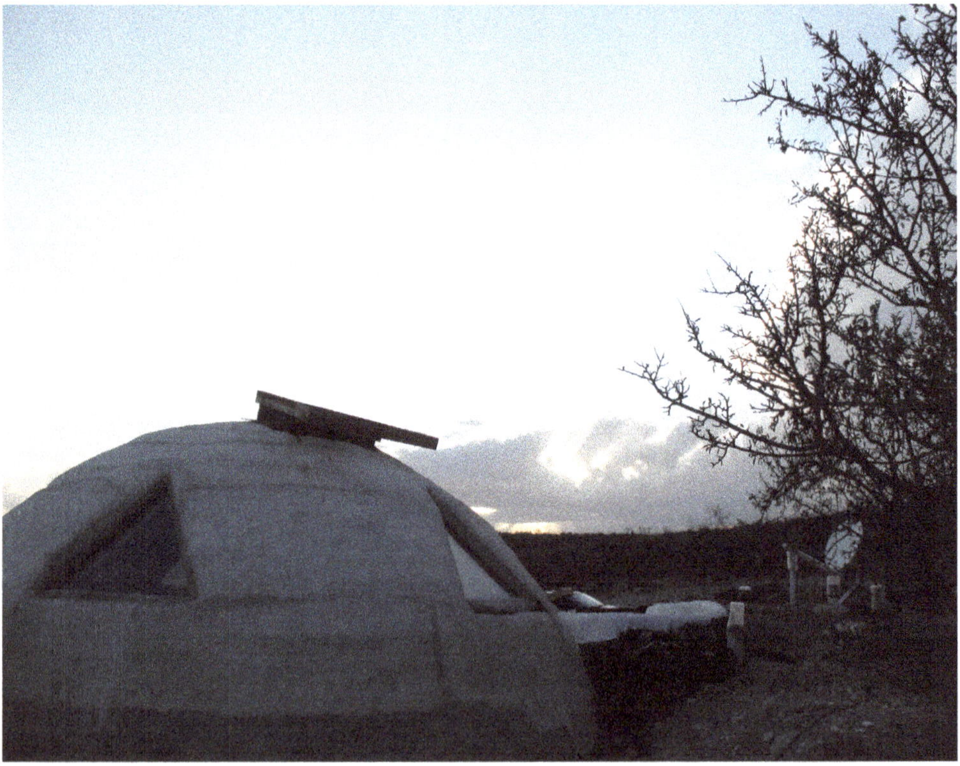

"My idea of interior design has changed hugely since moving to Spain and into an earthship – I think for the better!"

Mount Ninderry, Australia
Margot, Dan, Willoughby, Jack & Daisy

Approximately 100km north of Brisbane, Australia, you will find the gorgeous Sunshine Coast. Known for its beaches, surfing, eco-parks, nature reserves and glorious weather, the area is the third most populated in the state of Queensland. In the hinterland you will find towns such as Yandina, Nambour and Eumundi as well as the picturesque Mount Ninderry.

Surrounded by National Park and with many of the towns protected under heritage and by the Environmental Protection Agency, the region works hard to maintain its beauty. Local residents are passionate about eco-friendly life and the councils are very supportive of projects that will ensure sustainable living. Eco tourism is a fast-growing form of business throughout the Sunshine Coast with the hope that these residents can teach the tourists a thing or two about respecting and preserving their environment.

Have you ever wondered how a pair of architects might set about creating their family home? For two young architects, Margo and Dan, and their three children, designing and building a home of their own was an opportunity to put many of their ideas into practice.

"We were wanting to make a family home and we decided that we could get exactly what we wanted more economically if we built new rather than bought an existing house," Margo explains of the house they moved into back in 2006. "We love this area. It's a wonderful lifestyle – close to the

beach and surrounded by the bush – and we love being in a rural area and part of a small community."

When it came to designing the home, Margo does admit that their occupation gave them the upper hand. "Anyone can make a home like this, although we would advise that the use of an architect is paramount to achieve a comprehensive and detailed plan right from the start. Not only does this help from an economical perspective in the long term, but it also ensures the fundamentals of good passive design principles are used and it enables exposure to the latest in sustainable technologies."

Margo says that there were a number of design features and technologies employed to make this simple family home ecologically sustainable. "We planned rooms to have full solar orientation to the best aspect – the north in the southern hemisphere – for warmth in the cooler months and to ensure adequate lighting. We also included maximum cross ventilation to all rooms and all of these things greatly reduce your power needs.

"The roof overhang was calculated to shade glazing and cut out solar radiation during the warmer months, which helped keep the house cool. The footprint is small and the house was designed to suit increments of off-the-shelf materials to minimize waste. The house was actually prefabricated off site, in sections, by a modular construction company, and then assembled and completed on site. This also minimised waste and disturbance.

"Some of the technologies included rainwater tanks to provide a water supply for the entire house and an environmental waste water treatment system that used filtration and UV rather than chemicals to treat waste water. That also meant that we didn't have to connect into the main sewage system. We used the latest water-saving plumbing fixtures and power-saving electrical appliances and the roofs were pitched at the optimum angle and direction for harnessing solar energy for a time in the future when solar panels could be installed."

The rainwater tanks themselves were actually a special design feature that took the idea of 'multi-functional' to another level and made full use of the slope of the block. "The tanks were precast concrete providing thermal massing, with the walls of the tank being incorporated into the studio, ensuite and cellar spaces to the lower floor. A fourth precast tank was used as a plunge pool. We included structural glass portholes to the floors of the living area and bathroom to allow access to

the rainwater tanks. These can be lit up at night with a small reticulation pump providing delicate movements of light to the ceilings."

Margo found that perhaps the biggest deciding factor in the overall design was the location. "The land was very important. The house is in a semi-rural area, amongst a bush setting, and the house design needed to totally reflect its environment. It looks out to its surroundings from all angles and really connects with the outdoors. The land also dictated the design rationale. It is important to us to live in a natural space – so we wanted that feel of being surrounded by the bush with long views to the coastline. Our local council was fabulous and we had no trouble at all creating exactly the kind of home we wanted. They were very supportive of ecologically-sustainable design and that semi-rural area actually requires a fair bit of autonomy as there is no connection to main water or sewage."

Margo says that her and Dan have always had a great interest in the environment. "This was really enriched when we studied architecture at university. We feel so lucky to be in this industry and to be able to have a positive impact through good design. We also have fairly modern and minimalist tastes, and I think that suits well with eco living and design.

"Making eco-friendly choices can seem challenging because it often seems like the hard road rather than the easy one. However, even though the hard road is the one that takes longer, can sometimes cost a little more or take more researching, it always provides us with the best results in the end. I always think we should do what we can – no matter how small a thing it is. It all makes a difference! Start in your own backyard and go from there."

Outside of the busy schedules that come with having three kids, the family makes the most of their 'backyard' with visits to the beach and plenty of bushwalking. "It's a beautiful place to live and we do think Australia is one of the best places in the world to have a home. Mainly because of its natural beauty and the freedom and safety that we enjoy here." With views like these, that's certainly something they would be reminded of daily.

Check out more of Margo and Dan's work at www.sparksarchitects.com

"The land was very important.
We wanted that feel of being surrounded by bush
with views to the coast."

Kyoto, Japan
Bruce

On the island of Honshu, Japan, lies the city of Kyoto. Once the country's capital, Kyoto has a population of 1.5 million. Home to UNESCO World Heritage sites, imperial palaces and villas, temples, gorgeous scenery and plenty of restaurants and shops, it is a tourist favourite.

Kyoto sits atop a large natural water table that has provided the city with ample freshwater wells for centuries. However, due to large-scale urbanisation, the amount of rain draining into the table is dwindling and wells across the area are drying. In 1997, Kyoto hosted the UN conference on greenhouse gas emissions that resulted in the Kyoto Protocol treaty. Whilst this placed a spotlight on sustainability processes in Kyoto, and Japan in general, the country has fallen behind expectations due to a rapidly-growing population. Slowly but surely however, they are working together towards a more environmentally-friendly future.

British-born Bruce has only ever known a nomadic lifestyle. Growing up in the UK, Ireland, Nigeria and the USA, he headed to Japan in 1997 to conduct fieldwork for a PhD in anthropology. Now working for a university in Japan, he divides his time between his newly-adopted country, and his travels around the globe. In fact, Bruce admits it's his love of travel that is his greatest challenge when it comes to living in a sustainable way.

When it came to establishing his ideal home in Kyoto, Bruce was keen to create a passive house. "I wanted to design a house that ensured those living here could lead an eco-friendly life and not have to think about it," he says. "Because it's a passive house that is designed to work with the seasons, and all the appliances and systems are designed to work automatically to preserve and conserve energy, this is entirely possible. My real challenge in living an eco-friendly lifestyle is my international travel.

To some extent I use and support aviation companies trying to offset their carbon footprint and keep abreast of new technologies, but this is definitely a challenge for me."

The initial appeal of environmentally-friendly living started when Bruce was a student and spent some time living in a caravan with solar panels. "From that time, I always had a dream of building my own eco home," Bruce says. "Years later, I found myself living in the hills above Kyoto, and I started searching for the perfect piece of land. I wanted to build an eco dream house that would incorporate my years of research on ecological building and living principles. Once I selected the plot, I embarked on a four-year architectural and engineering project that involved teams of professionals, as well as members of the neighbourhood and good friends."

Bruce's home sits in the low mountains with the city of Kyoto on one side and Lake Biwa on the other. "Kyoto is a fascinating city," Bruce says. "It offers all the benefits of an ancient past – there are 14 UNESCO World Heritage sites within easy access of home – but it's also a modern city with many restaurants, business and entertainment districts. Lake Biwa is one of the world's ancient lakes with beautiful coastlines and scenery, inhabited and uninhabited islands and a wealth of surrounding farm-to-table and other eco friendly initiatives."

Bruce says Japanese life is conducive to an environmentally-friendly existence, and that locals – Japanese or not – are embracing a more sustainable way of life. "Ecological lifestyle principles are native to many aspects of the Japanese way of life," he says. "Of course, as is the case all over the industrialised world, many of these principles have been set aside in favour of modern time-or-cost saving approaches that dismiss time-honoured advantages and create more costly or unhealthy results in the long term. Fortunately, the ecological movement is in full swing in Japan today and indigenous methods of living are making a forceful comeback."

Having rented in Kyoto for 13 years, Bruce had been considering building for a while and he knew he wanted to embrace both the old philosophies and the new eco-friendly technologies available. On finding land in a picturesque location, he soon realised the plot itself was an important factor in the overall build. "The land was critical in terms of design," Bruce says. "Passive house design principles require south-facing windows in the northern hemisphere and therefore the orientation of the house on the land and the profile of the windows – or lack of them on the north side – was very important. Likewise, views of the surrounding mountain and the lake needed to be taken into account. A drone was used at the design stage to capture views from potential upper floor windows and terraces and satellite imagery of the surrounding mountain topography also played a role. The house shape and profile allow it to 'sit' within the landscape and enhance it, rather than stand out from it.

"When it came to construction and other elements, many factors were considered. The house is super insulated, with ultra-high performance rigid foam panels, in some areas up to 240mm thick, forming a sealed shell around the whole structure. The house itself is built using traditional Japanese timber framing techniques, using sustainable domestically-sourced Japanese cedar timbers for all posts and beams. The beams aren't solid timbers, but are layered and glued cedar planks, which are not only cheaper, but also more ecological in that large trees are not required for the manufacture.

"The roof overhangs are designed to let sun into the windows during winter and to keep the sun out during summer. All the doors and windows are double glazed, filled with insulating gas and have a special coating that allows heat in when the interior is cold and stops heat escaping when the exterior is cold."

Thanks to many clever innovations, Bruce says the house requires little or no heating unless the

outside temperature drops to less than six degrees Celsius. "The heat from human activity and the sun sustains the house down to these temperatures," Bruce explains. "When there is a succession of cloudy days, or the outside temperature drops below six, the house is heated by two industry-leading mini-split intelligent heat pumps. The super insulated nature of the house means once the desired interior temperature is reached, it can be kept at well below passive house standards – it uses approximately 200-400 watts for the whole volume of the house depending on the outside temperature. In summer, the same units cool and dehumidify the air for the whole house at around the same cost to cool a small, well-insulated apartment.

"I also have an energy recovery ventilator running 24/7. This replaces conditioned stale air with fresh air whilst maintaining the desired temperature and humidity with up to 90 per cent efficiency."

Bruce also combined new technologies with traditional concepts was the hot water system. "It works without the costs of storage, using tankless instantaneous electric heaters to provide hot water at a selectable temperature only when and where it's needed. The tankless heaters are positioned close to the output points to further conserve water and energy. The bathtub is made from Japanese cypress wood and is kept full of hot, bath temperature water during the winter using an immersion heater with a sensor and covered when not in use. The water is replaced every three to four days and, as per Japanese tradition, the body is washed outside the bath prior to using the tub for soaking rather than washing. So, water is conserved, energy usage is lowered and the bath is always ready."

Bruce says whilst he is finding it hard to find fault with his new eco home, there is one compromise he is still learning to come to terms with. "I enjoy cooking with natural gas, which isn't a sustainable resource. The induction cooking hobs and electric oven just isn't the same! For this reason, I keep two portable cassette-gas hobs on hand for the rare times I want to cook a stir-fry or use a wok. So, I suppose I use induction for 90 per cent of my cooking. Eventually, I hope a wood-fired oven will fulfill my need for a non-electric oven!"

When it comes to finding your own eco-friendly life, Bruce says he recommends the one thing that set him on his path: simple living in a simple space. "Experience eco-friendly life in some way and see what you think. Hire a mobile home or go camping and understand what components of your lifestyle require energy and how it is provided. Look into the old ways of life of the people of your region or country and see how they once designed and built houses. There is an archive of fascinating eco-friendly solutions which every culture has developed that partner with the natural world to create sustainable living. Stay in an eco home and understand how it feels and how it sits in the landscape and ecosystem of its surrounds."

To learn more about Bruce's building journey, visit his blog: www.housebuildjapan.blogspot.com

"I wanted to design a house that ensured those living here could lead an eco-friendly life and not even have to think about it."

Karoo, South Africa
Pietro, Amanda & Antonio

The nation of South Africa, like so many countries that have experienced rapid industrialisation and urbanisation, is dealing with many environmental issues, such as mining, overgrazing, intensive pesticide use, soil erosion, water and air pollution. The current government has recognised and acknowledged these problems however financial constraints and focusing on improving living standards and economic development has taken precedence.

Fortunately, individuals, small communities and companies are working hard at making a change. Just out of Cape Town lies the Karoo – a semi-desert natural region. Early adventurers and explorers defined it as an impenetrable barrier to Cape Town. The writer E. Palmer described it as "a frightening place of great heat, great frosts, great floods and great droughts." Today, a group of like-minded locals are developing nature reserves and game farms, turning the once-desolate Karoo into a tourist destination.

For Pietro, eco living is not just a part-time interest. It's literally his entire life. As well as working as founder and owner of Ecomo (www.ecomohome.com), a sustainable architectural firm that creates customised modular homes based on green design principles and modern, simple living, he also practices what he preaches: living with his family in one of his own creations.

"I've always had an interest in innovative design," Pietro says. "In today's world, it's not possible to be innovative and environmentally unaware at the same time. So, I think I've always had a passion and an interest in the environment. My wife, Amanda, however is an awesome inspiration in the way of day-to-day environmental sensitivity and good choices. Our home, and lifestyle, is certainly a culmination of these choices."

The family's eco-friendly home in the rural location of Karoo wasn't exactly planned. "A prospectus for the land popped up in my inbox one Sunday morning," Pietro explains. "I drove there in the pouring rain from Cape Town that same day and I fell in love. Just a few months later we purchased the plot.

"The land was very important. It would have been difficult to try and build and live in an environmentally conscious way if the lay of the land didn't support it. Because our home is situated in a nature reserve and has building and out-of-sight clauses, it made it almost easy to create the home and lifestyle we wanted. That's not to say that everyone wanting to live an environmentally sensitive lifestyle needs to live on land that offers this, however this is certainly how we wanted to live."

The two-bedroom family home was designed and built from scratch using Pietro's Ecomo housing (www.ecomohome.com). They are prefabricated, fully-customisable modular structures comprised of 'pods' that link together. The Karoo home is off grid with water sourced from a mountain spring. Black wastewater runs into a septic tank and the grey water goes into the garden. Rainwater is harvested to feed the planter boxes, a solar geyser is used for hot water and PV panels for electricity. The family grows its own vegetables and sources locally-grown organic eggs, meat and milk.

"From a design perspective, it's been fairly easy. We live with natural materials both in furniture pieces and soft furnishings such as linen and curtains. Again, if environmental awareness is a fundamental value one doesn't really feel compromised, because no other choice is appealing. If anything, I would say that we sometimes feel compromised because in order to utilise the sun's massive energy source, you need the money to install the best solar panels, converters and batteries. Without these, appliances such as washing machines and air conditioners – which can be powered sustainably – become impossible.

"The biggest challenge is time and expense. Because we are still in the minority by choosing to live this way, buying products and packaging that is environmentally friendly is more expensive. It's possible to make many products oneself; to grow one's own food for example, but this requires time.

Dealing with this becomes easier when environmental awareness is an unshakable value. This way, time is structured accordingly."

Despite feeling that eco-living should be more mainstream, Pietro has discovered many like-minded folk around his new neighbourhood – vast though it may be. "South Africa's Route 62 is a beautiful road," he says. "It winds its way for about 800 kilometres through the Klein Karoo and Groot Karoo. Along the way, one is taken through small hamlets and large farms. The sky seems endless and the land is vast. One of the tiny towns just off the R62 is Vanwyksdorp, which is made up of small homestead farms and people who have opted for a life of simplicity. Our plot is about 25km outside of Vanwyksdorp and the small surrounding farms have an ethical and environmental approach to working the land."

Pietro believes that there are many things you can do in order to make your own life a little more environmentally aware. "Compost your green waste – you can buy very small kitchen composters. Pot a few of your own veggies and herbs and start being aware of where your food is coming from. Be mindful of how you use water. These three very simple steps start bringing an awareness of how miraculous nature really is. There is no waste in nature. It is also fundamentally abundant. Watching green waste turn into nourishment for new life is hugely inspiring. Watching life come from a seed, some soil, sun and water is incredibly empowering. Life sustains life. There is a complete cycle and connecting to this cycle is the first step in becoming a part of the environment and not a part of destroying it."

"There is a complete cycle and connecting to this cycle is the first step in becoming a part of the environment and not part of destroying it."

Ho Chi Minh City, Vietnam
Tho

Ho Chi Minh City, formerlly known as and sometimes still referred to as Saigon, is the largest city in Vietnam. With over 10 million residents and rapidly expanding, it is anticipated the city will grow to over 30,000 square kilometres with a population of over 20 million by 2025. The global financial crisis in 2008 caused a property slump however the ongoing rise since that time has resulted in a push from the government to grow the city, and fast. This has meant that many of the colonial buildings the city was famous for have been razed to the ground to make way for brand new residences – many sky high – and the rapid urbanisation of the city is certainly straining environmental resources.

Affected by smog – Vietnam ranked among the top 10 countries with the worst air pollution in the 2012 Environmental Performance Index – as well as litter and polluted waterways, local residents are working hard to ensure that good decisions are made as the city expands. Builders and architects are creating innovative designs that allow eco-friendly homes to be built for not much more than the average house of the same size. It is this enthusiasm and call for change by residents that is now pushing local government to implement awareness programs and look at ways to grow the city in a responsible way.

Tho, a journalist working in Ho Chi Minh, is fortunate to find inspiration for his home in his daily work life. "I write about architecture and interiors for a magazine specialising in interior architecture," Tho explains. "I have also worked as an editor for a television program about architecture and interior design so I have a great appreciation for it."

Tho currently shares his home with his three cousins, who are studying, and he believes he has been able to create the perfect home, in the perfect location. "I bought a piece of vacant land, and worked with an architect, Nguyen Hoa Hiep of a21 Studio (www.a21studio.com.vn), to design

the home. I chose this place not only because it was a little out of the city centre – and the lower prices match my financial capabilities – but also because I love the fresh air and the tranquility. You definitely don't get that in the downtown area. I work in the centre and it only takes 30 minutes by motorcycle to get back to my quiet house and that rural feeling."

When working on the design with Nguyen, Tho had a few requirements outside of his love and knowledge of architecture, and his tight budget. The home, built in a new urban area, needed to work in harmony with the existing homes in the street. It needed to make clever use of space on its 40 square metre footprint and it also needed to look, feel and be 'green'.

The result is a home that a21 Studio refer to as 'The Nest'. Many of the basic elements of the house are made from recycled materials or existing materials that have been repurposed. The ground floor is completely open from both the front and the rear. This space houses a simple living room and kitchen that opens up to the small garden that surrounds the home. Colourful ceramic tiles cover every inch of the floor and also extend out beyond the shelter of the roof above. "The tiles were collected from various sources," Tho says. "Some were left over from friends' homes. I have used a lot of second-hand items in the design of the house – from the old wooden doors, to pieces of furniture and even the sanitary equipment was found at an old house. This not only reduced the construction cost, but also gave the house a unique look. There is a beauty that comes with age."

Because Tho was working to a tight budget, they decided on steel and metal sheets for construction as opposed to bricks and concrete. Whilst steel is not ideal from an environmental perspective, it is readily available on a local level and will not require any maintenance or replacing as the years pass. The steel columns and beams connect to the metal sheets and, over time, plants and vines will grow up and through, ensuring the home will eventually look like a green box. This will also help with cooling in Vietnam's tropical climate and will offer beautiful views from within the house.

The absence of walls in the property provides an abundance of natural light and ventilation. "We have really exploited natural light and wind," Tho says. "I don't use any air conditioning and the monthly cost for electricity consumption is very low – less than 300,000 Vietnam dong (approximately $15 USD) per month."

The house is located in a newly-developed area where the houses are built on a small scale.

"Overall, this was a cheap house. The cost for the building, garden, furniture, appliances, everything, came in at less than 350 million dong (just over $15,600 USD). I think it was almost too cheap for the great living space that I now have.

"Looking back, I realise that I didn't really have any challenges at all with the building process nor do I now with the house. Everything is very natural and I just go with the flow of life. With this house, depending on the weather conditions, I just make the necessary adjustments. Sometimes there are heavy rains and high winds which can make the downstairs area very wet – but the way it's designed means it doesn't matter if it all gets wet. If anything, the water gives it all a good clean which saves me some time mopping!"

Tho says that while he has an interest in environmental issues, he didn't set out originally to make his living space so environmentally friendly. "It proves how important a designer can be. Of course, I am very satisfied with the solutions and I have sourced products for my home that have been designed with both my lifestyle and this home and it's green footprint in mind.

"My advice to someone else setting out to do a new build is to really think carefully about your needs and find a good designer that is capable and who you can trust in."

With fewer expenses, a simple home and life out of the city centre, Tho admits that life is good. "I've got a job that I love, good friends and utilities to meet my needs – although I think my needs are simple and not much. I definitely believe that when you limit your needs, you are more likely to find satisfaction with life.

"My job isn't high pressure and it allows me a balance between work, relaxation and entertainment. In the morning, I go to work very early so that I am able to come home early too. As there is a new residential area near my home, I am able to take advantage of the facilities of the neighbourhood: swimming pool, gym and a few evenings during the week and at mass on Sunday I sing in the choir of a house Catholic church. I love listening to music, reading books and writing poetry and my house is an ideal space for these activities. My life is great."

"Over time, plants and vines will grow up and through and the home will eventually look like a green box. This will also help with cooling in Vietnam's tropical climate."

Margaret River, Australia
Michael & Britta

Margaret River is in the south west of Western Australia, almost three hours drive south of Perth. Known for its craft breweries and wineries, stunning surfing beaches and beautiful weather, the area is a popular tourist destination. With a population of around 5,000, the area receives more than half a million tourists annually.

In 2014 the Augusta-Margaret River Shire implemented a sustainability policy in an attempt to grow the region and provide a platform for tourism whilst improving local wellbeing. The shire also has a sustainable development department working on economy, waste, water and food. Local producers and ecovillages are also working hard to preserve and embrace Margaret River's natural beauty.

Perth-born architect, Michael, moved to Europe in the late 1980s. Whilst backpacking through Spain he met and fell in love with German-born, Danish-educated artist, designer and horticulturalist, Britta. "At the time I was living in London and Britta was in Hamburg so we had a long-distance relationship until I moved to Germany in 1990," Michael explains. "It was an auspicious time, being in Germany immediately after the reunification of the east and the west. Britta always felt as though she was born in the wrong country and was craving a milder climate and more sunlight, so in 1995 we moved to Margaret River."

Michael says living in Germany during the early 1990s was a great education in terms of environmental living. "The various authorities were always looking at ways to improve building standards, reduce energy consumption and recycle anything. We started consciously designing environmentally there and it was a great shock when we arrived in rural Margaret River in mid-1995. I guess, at that point, Australia was at least 15 years behind Germany in terms of environmental awareness, sustainability and the availability of eco products. I think Australia is still lagging behind

global trends in terms of sustainable building, but the gap has closed considerably. Moving to Margaret River meant having space so we could grow our own food – we originally moved to a two hectare property and had plenty of space to experiment with the best locations for the veggie garden, the fruit trees and the hen house. When we moved to our current 2,800 square metre plot, we applied all our knowledge from the previous place and we are now largely self-sufficient in food production. We have a cellar and most people would think, given we are in Margaret River, that it would be stocked with wine. There are one or two bottles of course, but it's mainly for food – preserves, pickles, jams and sauces."

The property isn't just a beautiful family home for Michael, Britta and their three-year-old English Springer Spaniel, Flot. The couple were keen to use their knowledge and creativity to design and build a wonderful, sustainable home. "For many years the local authorities, along with the state authorities, pushed for a by-pass road around the town centre in order to alleviate holiday traffic and encourage trucks out of the centre of town," Michael explains. "Unfortunately for us, our previous property lay in the way of this 'progress' and we were 'encouraged' to negotiate our way out. Our current home is really an example of turning a negative situation into a positive one.

"We started looking for a new plot and when we walked on to this one the rest, as they say, was history. It just spoke to us in so many ways. From there, we started the planning process, not just designing the house but really designing the whole site: what was going to go where and how it was going to be done. Two years later, after a lot of hard work and some heartache, we moved in."

At the same time Michael was dealing with ongoing negotiations with the road authority about the previous property, he was working on designing some homes for people from Perth. "I was really struggling to convince them that holiday homes don't need to be vast mansions," he says. "Mansions that have a bathroom for every bedroom or lots of bedrooms when there will only be two people there the majority of the time. So, when the opportunity arose for us to build our own place, we decided we really needed to practice what we were preaching. The result is a small footprint house designed exactly for our needs and the way we live and work. The house became a showcase for all things 'eco', in part so that I could show clients and demonstrate how sustainable design works, feels, smells and

operates. We went the whole hog. The Institute of Architecture in Western Australia awarded us with a Sustainable Architecture Award so I guess that really demonstrates our commitment to the project.

"If I had to choose one standout feature of the home, I would definitely say the glass roof over the dining room. It's fantastic. We have a reasonably moderate climate here that makes the glass roof very usable and we installed an automatic blind that we can roll out over the top on hot summer days. On winter days, it lets in valuable light and warmth. It passively drives the indoor climate of the whole house."

The passion to have things just so came at more of a cost than Michael perhaps would have preferred. "Because we were using this project as a bit of a workshop, and because we didn't want to compromise on any aspect of sustainability, there was an added cost," he admits. "A lot of that came in the form of added labour costs during construction. I guess the other aspect was the fact that a lot of the furniture was built-in and that, therefore, became a default part of the build cost. We applied the same standards of sustainability to the furniture as we did for the house construction. For example, the fabric in the soft furnishing is eco ethical wool, the filling is organic cotton, the timber finishing is natural oil and all the timber for the furniture was milled from trees on site. That makes things expensive, I guess, but what price can you put on compromise?

"When you allow conscious living to become the norm, there isn't really any challenge to it. It didn't happen overnight, there was an evolution and a gradual awareness. If you question everything along the way, then eventually you arrive at a style of living that you are comfortable with, within yourself."

It's those questions, Michael believes, that will allow anyone to move towards a more sustainable way of life. "Maybe start by asking: what impact do I have on my environment? Do I need to have that light on all the time and, if I do, then what kind of light is it? Could it be more efficient? Can I grow at least some of my food myself? If I can't, or it's not practical, what am I eating and where does it come from? Do I need to eat out-of-season foods (like tomatoes in winter that come from the other side of the world)? Do I need to drive a car, or can I walk or bike? There are many aspects of change that don't cost anything. There are other aspects of change that might have an initial cost, but cost less to operate or simply last longer and therefore don't need to be replaced so often. The little changes add up — and not just for that 'feel good' factor — quite often physically, emotionally and financially. For us, considering these things means we really have all we need."

See more of Michael's design work at www.sorensenarchitects.com.au

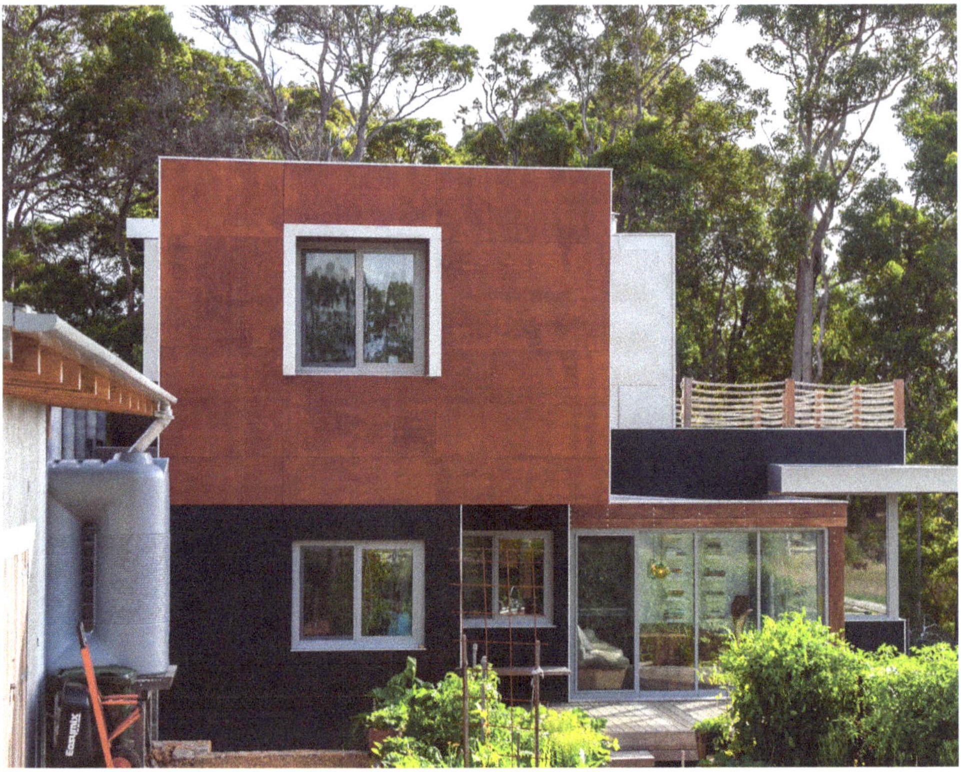

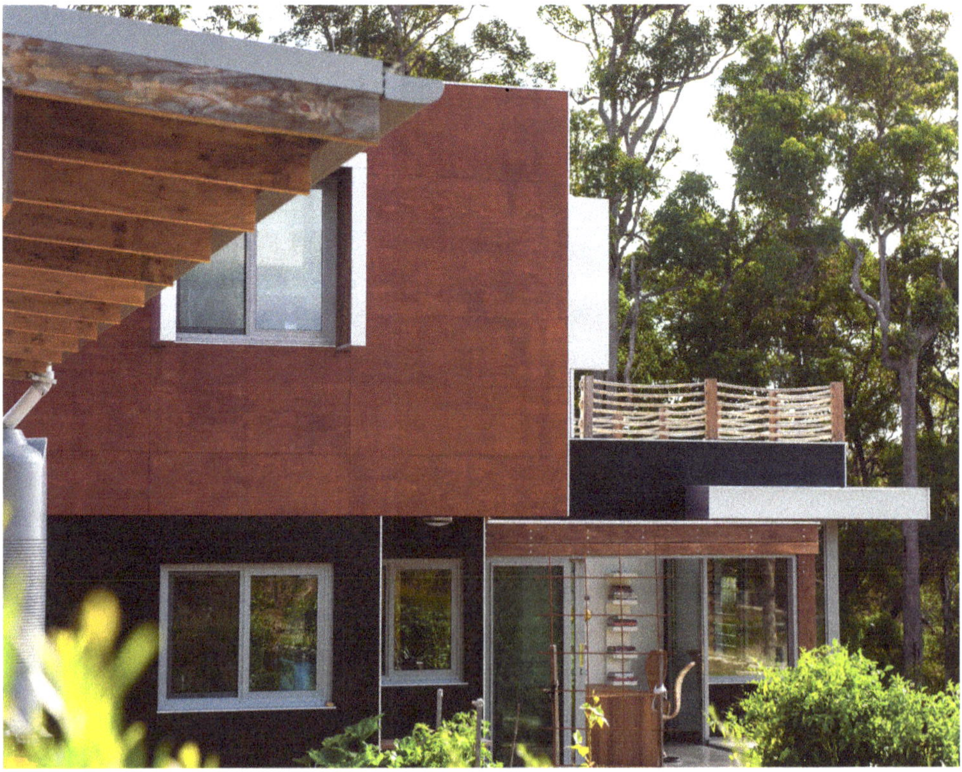

"Living consciously didn't happen overnight, there was an evolution and a gradual awareness."

St Dogmaels, Wales
Rachel

The country of Wales, in the southwest of Great Britain, was one of forerunners in the Industrial Revolution. The shift from an agricultural society into an industrial nation, meant a massive growth in income and population, but also some serious damage to natural resources. Over 200 years later, many of the country's extractive and heavy industries are gone or in decline and the nation is creating a new economy based around tourism and ethically-responsible trade – particularly in the more rural areas. In 2008, Wales made history by becoming the world's first nation to be awarded Fairtrade status.

To the very south west of Wales you will find the County of Pembrokeshire. The county is home to Pembrokeshire National Park – the only coastal national park of its kind in the United Kingdom. In 2011 it had 39 of its beaches recommended by the Marine Conservation Society. With a local community working hard to support renewable energy sources, including a newly installed submarine turbine, there are a number of sustainable businesses and projects within the region.

Rachel has lived on the same beautiful parcel of land in the north of Pembrokeshire for over 20 years and the connection she has with her area goes back even further. "My father is from Wales and I spent much of my childhood in the county, enjoying the beaches, hills, ancient rocks and landscapes," she says. "The land and coastlines offer a dramatic aesthetic and ancient wisdom that speaks to me.

"Over 20 years ago I came across this magical plot of land on a wooded hilltop looking over the Teifi estuary. Although I wasn't looking for land, I fell in love with it and heard the very next day it was for sale. I put in an offer and trusted that if it was meant to be, it would work out. After a year, I received notice it was possible."

Rachel spent four years living on the land in a small hut before she was granted planning permission to build a self-sustainable eco home. "My father left me an inheritance and, after a further four years, I began to build the house," she says. "In recent years, Pembrokeshire has become a hub for off grid and sustainable living, with a widespread commitment to a more low-impact way of living. Wales is a country with a focus on agriculture and farming. Eco homes and villages in the area now offer an additional focus on permaculture and living off grid. The community here is very well integrated with a growing movement of local markets and cooperative living.

"The site I found to build on was perfect. It was also one of the oldest sites in the village with an existing ruin. So, my house was built on a pre-existing slate slab on top of a hill with perfect land for a soakaway. Due to modern building control, we did have to dig out some of the slate and pour some concrete to appease our local officer! The local planning department was very supportive and sympathetic to the project and we were granted planning permission to build under a new policy, Agenda 21, supporting sustainable living and building. It was a learning process for all of us, but it did pave the way for more sustainable homes to be built locally."

This new build – Penwhilwr, meaning 'lookout' or 'watchtower' – was the first two-story, load-bearing straw bale home in the UK and the second in Europe. "It was a self-build project in collaboration with a pioneer women's straw bale building team headed by Barbara Jones," Rachel explains. "We ran courses and volunteer projects to build the house over three years with over 200 participants. The project was primarily managed by women. The intention was to use as many low impact and local materials as possible, with timber from local woodlands and straw bales from within the vicinity. Apart from some foundations, there was no use of concrete, with lime and clay being the primary plasters and mortars. Many traditional techniques were applied along with the latest straw bale techniques.

"The gift of building through courses and volunteering meant that many people were able to experience, and learn for themselves, how to build a straw bale home. As a result, many homes have been built around Europe using the same techniques."

Rachel says the experience of the shared build gave her more than just a place to live. "It was an inspiring, nourishing and empowering experience to build in a way that communities in the past once did. All members of the community could be involved in the process, from children through to elders, some with experience and some with no experience. There was always a task for everyone, even if it was tea making!"

The house is curved and the design was based on the geometry of nature. "Curves seem to offer conflict-free zones and sit well in our vibrant woodland," Rachel says. "It is very much in harmony with its surroundings. It wasn't an expensive home to build. Being load-bearing, it saved on a considerable amount of carpentry and timber, as usually straw bale homes are built with a frame and filled in with the straw. The load-bearing design meant we only required straw bales for the structure, along with locally-sourced hazel stakes. The inside was plastered with clay, which was mainly free and locally sourced, and then lime plaster on the outside, which was more of an investment. It's certainly something that most people could afford to build.

"The house is powered by the sun and the wind, so I have to watch my power usage and I am at the mercy of the elements in many ways. Of course, it can be a blessing to turn off the power

and listen, or go for a walk in nature on a day when the sun and wind are low. Perhaps the greatest challenge for me is getting the wood ready to fuel the house each winter. The house is fuelled by a wood burner with wood cut from the woodland and it is often quite a job to get it cut and seasoned in preparation for the winter ahead. I also live up a footpath, which means everything must be carried up to the house."

Rachel admits she couldn't live any other way now she's experienced life in her new home. "I have always loved being in nature and, through the years, coming home to Wales from the cities I've lived in was like coming home to my true self. I used to step into my little hut and shed all the baggage of life and surrender to a kinder and more vibrant way of living. The building of this house changed my life beyond words.

"It restored my faith in humanity. To build with, and share the experience with, so many good-hearted folk from so many walks of life healed something inside. An aching to be part of something authentic, kind and harmless. It also anchored a deeper commitment to living in this way and to share the beauty of such a life with others. I practice and share yoga and meditation here and also retreats in sustainable and pranic living, as well as women's retreats. It's a fairly contemplative life here and I love to offer this opportunity to others, so the house is also now available to rent on AirBnb.

"For anyone wanting to live a more environmentally-friendly lifestyle, I would suggest spending more time in nature. Walking, being and listening in nature usually provides the answers required for stepping into such a way of life. Also, meeting with other inspirational eco lovers and joining in projects to support nature and the land helps to create new possibilities, connection and support."

Learn more about Rachel's home and her retreats at www.quietearthretreat.co.uk

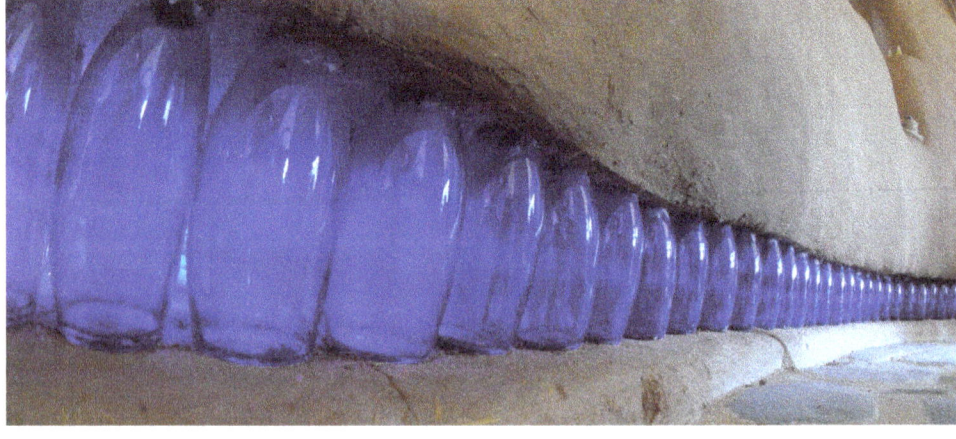

"The building of this house changed my life beyond words. It restored my faith in humanity. To work with so many good-hearted folk healed something inside."

Carmel-by-the-Sea, USA
Mica & Laureen

Carmel-by-the-Sea (or just Carmel, as it's known) is a small coastal town in the central west of California. Just over 500km north of Los Angeles, its mild Mediterranean climate, beautiful beaches and artistic history makes it a popular tourist destination. With a population of just under 4,000 the town has historically pursued a strategy of planned development to enhance its natural coastal beauty and retain its character.

New builds must be built around existing trees and the small village has no streetlights or parking metres. Carmel was incorporated in 1916 and as early as 1925 the town adopted a clear vision for its future. In fact, records from the city council at the time state it is 'primarily, essentially and predominantly a residential community' and it now regularly hosts delegations from cities around the world seeking to understand how it manages to retain its authenticity. In the waters around Carmel you will find four major marine conservation areas where the marine life is just as fiercely protected as the development of the town.

Interestingly, Mica and Laureen never actually set out to create an 'eco-home' however the results of their beautiful property are proof that you can live your dream, and be kind to the environment at the same time.

The couple had always loved Carmel and had a long-held dream to one day call it home. "We fell in love with the place in the late 80s, early 90s," Mica explains. " We never really thought it would be a reality. As we approached our 25th wedding anniversary, and there were many challenges with the economy, we thought maybe we could afford a little cottage here. We actually closed on the home on the day of our anniversary!

"Originally, we just planned for a place with excellent insulation." Working with local builder, Rob Nicely, and architect, Justin Pauly, the couple was quickly educated about the benefits of a passive home. "Rob and Justin listened well and began to guide us through the many decisions one makes when creating a home…and the laundry list of choices. The idea of a passive house was intriguing. The thought of building a home in an airtight envelope was tremendous and the decisions we made, with their help, seemed obvious. Use less energy. Leave a smaller footprint. Save water. Monitor your consumption. Protect the environment."

Architect, Justin, explains that there were several steps taken in the design of the structure to create a passive home. "Proper solar orientation and a fairly compact building were a great start but we tried to pursue many technical details as well. For example, we filled all of the stud bays with foam insulation and wrapped the entire envelope of the house – walls and roof – with a layer of rigid insulation. We used Loewen triple-paned windows with really solid u-values and a HRV system to both heat the home and circulate fresh air throughout the structure. With a tight building envelope, good air quality can be a concern so we wanted to address that. We also pursued advanced framing techniques that not only minimised the use of wood but also the amount of thermal bridging in the building envelope."

From a design perspective, Justin says that nothing they did pushed the envelope in terms of code compliance, so they had no trouble with the planning commission. "Unfortunately," he admits, "they didn't seem overly interested either."

Justin says that it was important to all of them that no great compromises were made in order to achieve their goals – especially financially – and Mica agrees. "While some things were more expensive, you save in other areas," Mica says. "We don't have a heater, or an air conditioner, so we are saving in those ongoing expenses. However, better insulation costs more, as do better windows, and eco-friendly building supplies such as paint, flooring and a zinc roof all add up. What you end up with certainly outweighs the alternative though. Our home has clean air coming in and exiting every few seconds and being airtight means it's also bug-free. Rob and Justin didn't push the eco-friendly movement upon us – they simply asked questions and gave us options and together we seemed to make eco-friendly decisions without realising it."

Mica says that he and Laureen have thought about what they would do differently and they can't name a single thing. "Our wood floors are 100-year-old repurposed red and white oak with bug holes and knots and we love it. The walls are plaster, which not only look beautiful but are also easy to maintain. We wanted a Wolf Range, and that was potentially an issue due to venting, but Rob diligently worked to seek out ways that wouldn't compromise the passive pathway and made it happen. There's not a thing we would change.

"For people starting out, I would recommend they do what we did. Look online and ask around at builders and architects and see what they're doing and what others are saying about them. We found Rob at Carmel Building and Design first and when we read about his philosophy we were really interested. When we met with him, he asked us how we live and what's important to us. He really listened and we understood that he was building our home, not just a house. It was Rob who brought out the environmentalist in us – although I think that it was always who we were. Then Rob brought in Justin – an architect he'd always wanted to work with – and they were a match made in heaven. They complimented each other perfectly."

"Rob and I really looked at both the short term and long term impacts of the building," Justin says. "We were really focused on energy efficiency and energy usage, but we were also conscious of the materials that we were using and ensuring they didn't have a big footprint."

The result is a home that Mica and Laureen are 100 per cent satisfied with, in a pocket of the world that they adore. "Carmel is special," Mica says. "It's not at all pretentious and it has such a great energy. We love its history and we also love how dog friendly it is. The beach, the stores and the restaurants all embrace the furry kids! We're just a short walk to the beach in one direction and the shopping and restaurants in another, with beautiful oak trees to our rear. We just love Carmel.

"We've travelled to many countries and have lots of favourite places in the world, but we do take pride in knowing where home is. We love the outdoors, animals and nature and when we aren't working we like to hike. As California natives we know water is precious and turning off the water, turning off the lights and being responsible with our resources is something we've been raised with. We do all we can to be mindful of our responsibility to care for the earth. Recycle, reuse and cherish our resources."

> *"Originally, we just wanted a place with excellent insulation...but the idea of a passive house was intriguing. Use less energy. Leave a smaller footprint. Protect the environment."*

Lima, Peru
Patrick, Marina, Mathias & Oliver

Peru sits alongside the Pacific Ocean in western South America with Ecuador and Colombia to the north, Brazil to the east and Bolivia and Chile to the south. An extremely biodiverse country, Peru has habitats ranging from arid plains in the west, the mountainous Andes in the north down to the southeast, and the tropical Amazon in the east. Rich with history, tourists flock to Peru to see such sites as the ancient citadel of Machu Picchu. In the central west you will find the capital, Lima, with almost 10 million residents. Lima was the destination for the 2015 UN conference on climate change which generated a great deal of discussion on creating a more sustainable future for the country.

The Lurín district is one of three valleys in Lima and the Lurín River is a system of ancient canals. The areas surrounding the river are green and excellent for cultivation. Although it rarely rains in the area (less than 2.4 inches per year), there is a thick fog, which the locals call 'Serena'. The mist drops and moistens the entire area, filling the canals and keeping the landscape rich and green. Lima, however, relies on water from wells and rivers that flow from the Andes, meaning water conservation is an issue the city must deal with as the population grows.

In a green strip of land next to the Lurín River, right where the 'Serena' falls, is a magical house that, from a distance, could well have been built hundreds of years ago. It belongs to a nature-loving, creative family who spent many years travelling between Europe and South America before finally settling down. Patrick, a visual artist, and his wife, Marina, an urbanist and university teacher, were originally from Peru and their plan was always to someday come home. "We lived in Geneva for 11 years and always had the idea of coming back to our country and building the home of our dreams,"

Patrick says. "We acquired the land whilst we were still living in Europe, so by the time we headed back to Peru we already had this project in mind."

Patrick admits that 'eco living' isn't a term he identifies with, but his connection to the land and the respect he has for his environment indicates this home was created with great sensitivity to nature. "I guess we've always been interested in taking care of our environment and caring for our natural resources," Patrick says. "From the beginning the setting of the house was very important to us. It is located in a sort of belvedere looking over the valley. We spent a couple of nights camping in the spot to hear the sounds of nature and observe the position of the sun so the house would be in the best possible setting. The process of building definitely contributed to us being more aware of our natural surroundings and trying to take care of it."

The family employed a local architect, Marina Vella (www.marinavellarquitecta.com), who dealt with builders in the area and talked about the possibilities of the materials. "The house was inspired by local architecture of the area and the materials and flora here," Marina explains of the build. "We worked closely with a local builder who had extensive knowledge of traditional techniques. Peru has an ancient culture of both technical knowledge and use of sustainable materials in specific areas. Unfortunately, like so many other parts of the world, people want 'quick' and 'modern' and before long all our homes are the same and made of brick, cement and iron. What we wanted to achieve with this home was the look of a contemporary project, using traditional techniques and materials."

Marina says other sustainable ideas were used to ensure the house didn't rely on resources as much as many modern properties do. "The high ceilings and cross ventilation, as well as using materials like stone and earth, are helpful with avoiding artificial heating and cooling. The house was designed compactly but with 3.2 metre ceiling heights and views to all sides, allowing good natural light and ventilation, so the atmosphere seems much bigger than the actual footprint. Having care with scale is important. People imagine very large areas when, really, they're not needed. The house also has neither a front nor backyard so there are no dead zones inside or out.

"One should investigate, talk to the locals, and see how materials work. It's about being creative with techniques and solutions. The challenge was about taking everything we know and responding to a current way of living," Marina explains.

"It took us a year to build, but it was a year full of learning experiences and discovering the possibilities of traditional materials," Patrick says of the building process. "The house is mainly built out of stone, adobes and wood. These natural materials absorb heat during the day to keep the house warm at night, and absorb the cold at night to keep the house fresh during the day. We use wastewater for watering our plants. We have a vegetable garden and all our organic waste is used for compost. I do believe however that it's an attitude, more than the house itself, that makes a place 'eco-friendly'."

Patrick admits that often progress invades nature. "We see big walls being built up by new owners to make condo projects or private houses that don't integrate with nature at all," he says. "It destroys the very beauty of it. It's frustrating and we often talk to local people in the valley about being aware of the value of nature and their landscape. Unfortunately, there's a lack of regulations from the government to protect nature and it's very hard to make changes in that sphere.

"Lima is a huge, amazing city. It's full of history, but it has a lot of problems as well. We wanted to live near Lima, but far away from the noise of the city, so this place was ideal for us. We are surrounded by nature, a river flows below and we have a clear sky and beautiful weather year round. Home is definitely where your heart — or your family is — so I could be anywhere in the world as long as they were there too. I do love the ancient living culture that Peru has — be it on the coast, mountains or in the rainforest. It's amazing.

"Unfortunately, there is a huge education gap between the different social classes here and there's a lot of work to be done in order to teach people to respect and love their environment. My advice to people is to try and be a little more conscious of the environment and to treat it as a living creature. Be grateful for nature and nurture the land we live in."

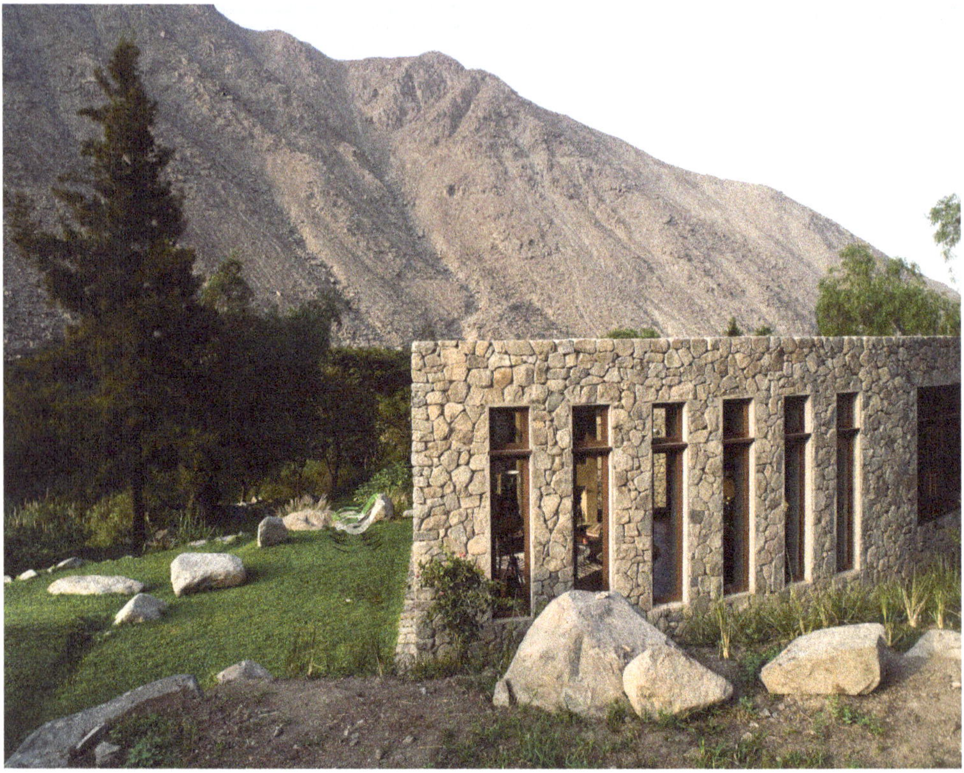

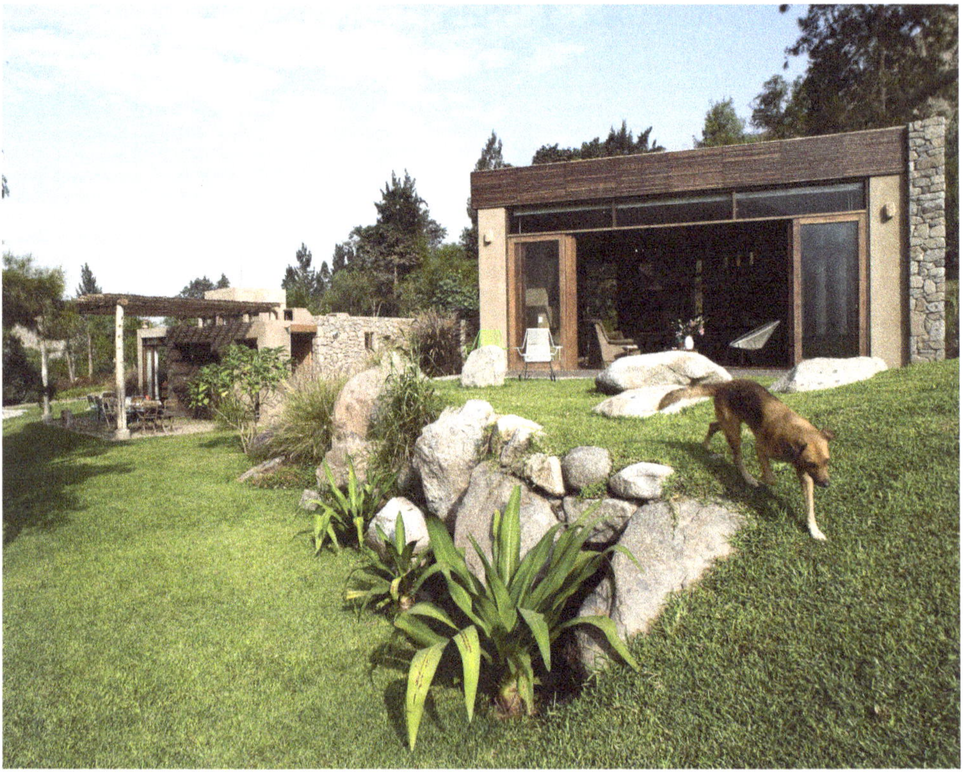

"We spent a couple of nights camping in the spot to hear the sounds of nature and observe the sun, so the house would be in the best possible setting."

Photo Credits

Cover image: (Sandhorøy, Norway) **Ingrid Marie Hjertefølger**

Page 3: (Lima, Peru) **Carmen Ravago**

Pages 4 & 5: (Watercolour World Map) **Pavlo Raievskyi**

Page 6: (Pipestem, USA) **Nick Olsen**

Page 7: (Sandhorøy, Norway) **Ingrid Marie Hjertefølger**

Pages 8, 9, 10, 11, 12, 13, 14, 15: (Daylesford, Australia) **Mara Ripani**

Pages 16, 17, 18, 19, 20, 21, 22, 23, 24, 25: (Sandhorøy, Norway) **Ingrid Marie Hjertefølger**

Pages 26, 27, 28, 29, 30, 31, 32, 33: (Castleton, Canada) **Riley Snelling**

Pages 34, 35, 36, 37, 38, 39, 40, 41: (Pipestem, USA) **Marcus Constantino**

Pages 34, 35, 36, 37, 38, 39, 40, 41: (Pipestem, USA) **Half Cut Tea**

Pages 34, 35, 36, 37, 38, 39, 40, 41: (Pipestem, USA) **Nick Olsen**

Pages 34, 35, 36, 37, 38, 39, 40, 41: (Pipestem, USA) **Naomi Huober**

Page 42: (Family image - Queenstown, New Zealand) **Laura Shallcrass**

Pages 43, 44, 45, 46, 47, 48, 49: (Queenstown, New Zealand) **Build Me (www.buildme.co.nz)**

Pages 50, 51, 52, 53, 54, 55, 56, 57: (Almeria, Spain): **Laura Davies**

Page 57: (bottom image - Almeria, Spain) **Kevin Borman**

Pages 58, 59, 60, 61, 62, 63, 64, 65: (Mount Ninderry, Australia) **Jesse Lockhart-Krause & Dan Sparks**

Pages 66, 67, 68, 69, 70, 71, 72, 73: (Kyoto, Japan) **Bruce White**

Pages 74, 75, 76, 77, 78, 79, 80, 81: (Karoo, South Africa) **Pietro Russo**

Pages 82, 83, 84, 85, 86, 87, 88, 89: (Ho Chi Minh City, Vietnam) **Hiroyuki Oki**

Pages 90, 91, 93, 94, 95, 96, 97: (Margaret River, Australia) **Tim Swallow**

Pages 98, 99, 100, 101, 102, 103, 104, 105: (St Dogmaels, Wales) **Rachel Shiamh**

Pages 106, 107, 108, 109, 110, 111, 112, 113: (Carmel-by-the-Sea, USA) **Rob Yagid of Taunton Press**

Pages 114, 115, 116, 117, 118, 119, 120, 121, 122, 123: (Lima, Peru) **Carmen Ravago**

Want more?

Homes Of The World

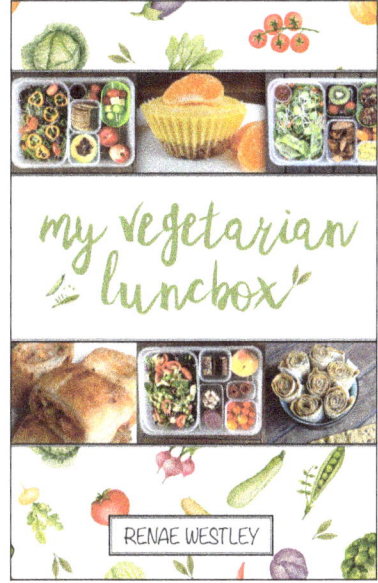

Food

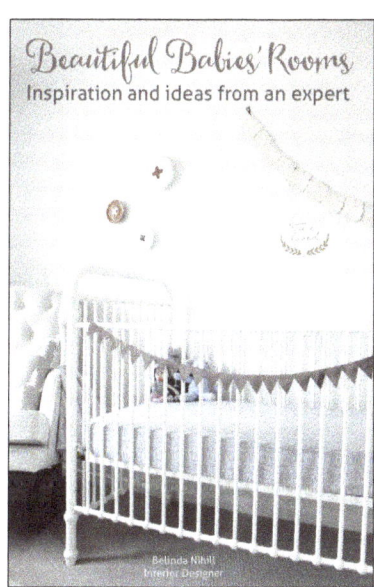

Interiors

Artist Spaces

www.oftheworldbooks.com
or your favourite online bookstore

www.ingramcontent.com/pod-product-compliance
Lightning Source LLC
Chambersburg PA
CBHW040335300426
44113CB00021B/2756